DEEP IN THE FAMILIAR

DEEP IN THE FAMILIAR

Four Life Rhythms

▲▼▲▼

JOAN CANNON BORTON

THE
PILGRIM
PRESS
Cleveland

For Ross, my dad,
with whom I share the love of words

For Cam, my husband,
with whom I share the love of silence

Excerpt from "The Companionable Dark" from *Little Girls in Church* by Kathleen Norris © 1995; reprinted by permission of the University of Pittsburgh Press. From *A Seven Day Journey with Thomas Merton* © 1992 by Esther de Waal; published by Servant Publications, Box 8617, Ann Arbor, MI 48107. From *The Sign of Jonas* by Thomas Merton; used by permission of Harcourt, Inc. From "A Time for Grieving, Rejoicing," by Rosemary Haughton; printed in the *My View* column of the *Gloucester Daily Times*, April 12, 1997. From "Solitude" and "Wilderness" by Beverly Williams; used by permission.

Scripture quotations unless otherwise noted are from the New Revised Standard Version Bible, copyright © 1989 by the Division of Christian Education of the National Council of the Churches of Christ in the United States, and are used by permission.

The Pilgrim Press, Cleveland, Ohio 44115
www.pilgrimpress.com

Printed in the United States of America on acid-free paper

06   05   04   03   02   01   5   4   3   2   1

Library of Congress Cataloging-in-Publication Data

Borton, Joan C., 1938-
    Deep in the familiar : four life rhythms / Joan Cannon Borton.
    p. cm.
    Includes bibliographical references.
    ISBN 0-8298-1408-6 (alk. paper)
    1. Christian women – Religious life. I. Title.

BV4527.B67 2001
248.8'43 – dc21

                    2001016390

CONTENTS

ACKNOWLEDGMENTS

The reflections that follow come out of solitude and community. I am deeply grateful to the women and men who have shared their experience with me and whose words are included in *Deep in the Familiar*.

My family have all contributed to this book through their words and their ongoing support. I want to thank each one of them: Ross Cannon, my father, whose words at key moments have kept me on track; Mary Cannon, my mother, who has read every word of my many manuscripts; and my children, Jim Borton, Jenni McIntosh, and Lawrie Williams, who have shared their experience and encouraged me all along the way. My husband, Cam Borton, has shared his life with me for the past forty years. I have dedicated this book to him with deep gratitude for his humor and playfulness, for his presence in crisis and in calm, and for his love of silence.

Gloria Masterson skillfully worked with me on many drafts as my gifted writing coach. Her understanding of my voice and her belief in me kept me going through the writing process. Lynn Runnells has provided a sacred space for me to play with ideas and to be guided by the Spirit as I have participated in her Creativity and Spirituality Workshop.

Included in the following pages are the words and experiences of people who have shared themselves with me over the past ten years. I want to thank them for their contributions to my life and to this book: Pat, Jan, Nicole, Rebecca, Sister Jeanne Marie, Jim, Cecily, Mary, Ross, Ann, Bev, Margaret, Martha, Wendy, Carole, Beth, Patti, Jean, David, Lawrie, Elaine, Nancy, Liz, Lyn,

Deborah, Peggy, Dan, Jane, Linda, Barbara, Sandra, Lynn, Helen, Jenni, Annemarie, Kathleen, Barbara, Sarah, Martha, Sister Donald, Nancy, Rosemary, Gloria, Jill, Camilla, Helen, Eloise, Kris, Jane, Susan, Carol, and Courtney.

The groups of women who used the manuscript for study and reflection gave me invaluable feedback. I thank Suzanne, Jean, Patti, Bev, Laurie, Sandy, Joanna, Pat, Dodie, Elaine, Jane, Jill, Sarah, Jan, Linda, Joan, Jaci, Patty, Betsy, Betty, Deb, Liz, Mary Jane, Sue, Lyn, Linda, Anita, Martha, and Peggy. I am also grateful for the constructive feedback from three readers of my manuscript: Rebecca Koch, Evelyn Clark Farbman, and Anne Ryan, and for the technical support of Camilla Ayers, David Clark, Tom Ryan, and Jim Schell, who have seen me through many crises. Thank you.

In 1994 the members and friends of the First Congregational Church in Rockport, Massachusetts, gave us the gift of sabbatical time to be in three contemplative settings: Transfiguration Monastery in Windsor, New York; Pendle Hill: A Quaker Center for Study and Contemplation in Wallingford, Pennsylvania; and the Hermitage of the Dayspring, Kent Hollow, Connecticut. It was during this time of rest and replenishment that I began to explore the call to go deep in the familiar. For this experience of forest time, I am most grateful. I also give thanks for Nancy, who introduced me to the forest paths of Cape Ann, and for other friends who walked with me in many different ways during my years there.

Most recently I want to thank those who walked with me through the process of publishing this book. Kim Sadler, my editor at The Pilgrim Press, had the vision and creativity to help shape the manuscript. I am also grateful to Christine Finnegan for her sensitivity and skill as copyeditor and to John Eagleson for artistically implementing it all and answering my many questions.

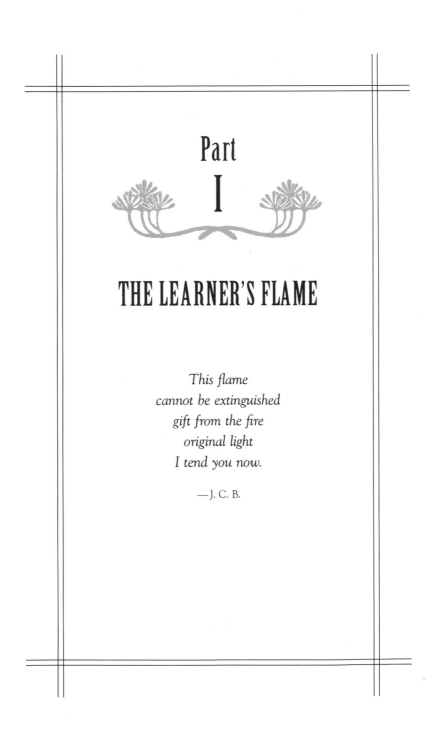

Part
I

THE LEARNER'S FLAME

This flame
cannot be extinguished
gift from the fire
original light
I tend you now.

—J. C. B.

GOING DEEP IN THE FAMILIAR

I lived at a crossroads in a Midwestern town during my childhood and adolescence. It was the era when Catholics and Protestants went to separate schools. We Protestants always thought that the "Catholic kids" were really tough. And I can imagine all sorts of things that they thought about us.

One afternoon at that crossroads as a nine-year-old, I was trying to fix my bike chain. It had come off the sprocket. "We can fix it," I said to my friend Zay. I forced it over the spiky gear. Suddenly, the middle finger of my left hand was caught under the greasy chain, pressed between two sharp points. I tried to get it out by turning the pedal, only to feel the crush of the chain as it tightened and cut into my finger.

Zay ran for her father. Mrs. Sorrenson came out. She lived upstairs and was taking care of my brother and me. A crowd gathered. I cried.

Zay's father came and knelt down beside me to release the chain. "Mrs. S." held me and some high school kid said, "I'll drive you to the hospital."

My finger throbbed as I sat on the front seat of his car between him and Mrs. S. Leaning into her soft body, my eyes focused on a small statue on the dashboard. Later, when I asked her about it,

3

she said, "He's Catholic, you know." "Then," I said, "they can't all be bad."

In my fortieth year I was at another crossroad. For health reasons I had to resign from teaching in our local elementary school, a career that I thought was to be my vocation. The oldest of our children was about to enter college. I needed to find another way to help support our family.

I wanted to explore two roads previously not taken, ministry and counseling, so I began with a seminary course in religious education. Maria Harris was a Catholic professor at a Protestant seminary. Her enthusiasm for the work of Gabriel Marcel, a French Christian existentialist, was contagious. It was the late seventies when she introduced me to his ideas about the spiritual journey and our human condition as travelers on the way. This phrase spoke to my experience. The assignment to write a spiritual biography challenged me to reflect on my journey.

In my life review I became aware of how essential my journal has been over the years—a companion as I have traveled; a vehicle for soul work on the way. Maria Harris rekindled my desire to teach what I loved. So I created a journal course and began offering journal workshops and retreats which opened the way to my becoming a licensed mental health counselor.

While I was training to become a therapist, I also worked at our local bookstore. On occasion people would come in to ask if we had "any Christian books." I had difficulty knowing how to answer the question. From my crossroads experiences I had learned that labeling limits possibility. I found myself responding with words like these: "We have a fine selection over there (pointing to the Religion, Philosophy, and Inspiration section) where you will find the writings of Thomas Merton and others." I think I was reaching toward someone whose life and work said it is possible to move beyond labels and at the same time go deeply into the mystery of the Holy One in one's own tradition.

I find labels restrictive. After eight years as a mental health counselor, I stopped working with insurance. It required a diagnosis for people who in many cases were doing soul work. They were becoming aware of themselves as "travelers on the way," and they wanted me to accompany them for a while as they walked their journey. I had learned that diagnostic labels provide no room for the unfolding mystery that is each person.

Deep in the Familiar draws on the living of my days and on the experiences of women and some men who have shared their lives with me. The process of going deep in the familiar has several levels of meaning for me. On one level, it is a way to work in the counseling process or with one's own personal growth through a journal. It also describes a path for spiritual practice. This series of reflections offers you, the reader, a way to be with your journey, a way to honor yourself as a sacred work in process.

Going deep in the familiar is also a way to go beneath known and well-worn labels to touch the roots of others at a level below the surface of life. Groups of women who have used this book together have found this to be so. In the depths there is much that is common. It is where we are all ultimately fed by the underground stream of living water that is the Holy One. In this deep river, our traditions and treasures from the Spirit merge and become available to all, for in the depths we touch mystery.

We are all travelers on the way home. This pilgrimage—for me and for many women—is taking place right where we are and the place where we are is often in the midst of other people and their lives. As caregivers and wage earners, involved with and connected to others, we are so engaged in relationships or work that we fail to recognize our own experience as a soul journey. We do not see our daily lives as the means by which we are living our way into the heart of mystery, our true home.

In my work as a mental health counselor, I learned that the Greek root word for therapy, *therapaeia*, means "attention of the kind one devotes to sacred mysteries."[1] The need for attending to each other in this way is great. As women we are often painfully aware of the needs of our own loved ones, friends, coworkers, our fractured human family, and this fragile planet Earth. When we recognize one another and the natural world as sacred, we become aware of the unfolding mystery that is at the heart of all creation. This kind of devotion draws on all of our resources.

Often we feel the needs of others so strongly that they take all our journeying energy and there is none left to devote to ourselves. As we live our daily lives—with all the changes and challenges of our fast-paced world—it becomes imperative that we devote this kind of attention to ourselves as well, in order to find a balanced way to walk our individual and collective paths.

There are many different ways for finding and regaining balance. For fifteen hundred years, balance has been the core of Benedictine spirituality. The wisdom underlying the practices of this Christian monastic community is available to all of us. As a Protestant Christian, I have been exploring what is called the Benedictine Way. I have found encouragement to develop spiritual practices that I can bring to my life in community from contemporary interpreters of the Rule of Saint Benedict. They present the importance of listening to God through our everyday life in order to be open to change and creative possibility while being present and committed to the here and now.

In our everyday lives as women, there are some elemental rhythms which can help create a dynamic kind of balance when we recognize and honor them with our attention. An ancient

Hindu tradition considered the need for these elements, but saw them in a linear progression of life phases.

Originally describing the experience of men in an Indian culture, the life stages began with the student or learning years, which were followed by the householding years, a time to establish oneself in work ("the marketplace") and family ("the village"). Later, when a man saw the sons of his sons, he left his family and possessions and went into the forest to live as a hermit. Through various spiritual practices and reflection during that forest time, he would come to the experience of mystical union and "enter the fourth and final stage of life, wandering the land, emancipated from all desire and suffering."[2] This kind of emancipation from the human condition is not the goal for my life, nor is an ordered progress from stage to stage possible for most people in contemporary life. However, these stages have parallels in my life as a woman in the twenty-first century.

The "student" is alive and well in me every time I become excited about learning something new or persevering with a project that requires my focus. The student or learner connects me with the creative energy at my core. I am a "householder" when I am creating a home, involved in family, work, and community. "Time in the forest" speaks to my need for solitary time apart from my householding life.

For some women, leaving all behind has been a way to discover union with the Holy One. For others, the way is not to detach for a long period of time, but to find solitude for shorter experiences of forest time. For me time apart makes possible a deeper awareness of the Eternal and my sense of oneness with all creation. It often provides space for perspective, enabling me to sort things out so that I can make choices that are authentic for me. This may be a form of emancipation, because through this process I become, in Saint Irenaeus's words, "more fully alive."

Then it seems possible to "return to the village" replenished and more aware of my union with God right in the midst of my daily life. Going deep in the familiar is one way to realize the Incarnation, God in our midst, day by day.

The Hindu life phases offer four themes that reoccur as essential rhythms that weave in and out of our lives as women. I have found it helpful to explore these myself and also with the women with whom I work. This book combines my reflections on these themes and the words and experiences of a number of women. The nature of the writing is personal. One woman who contributed to this project commented on the four sections of the book: "The images, tending the flame, going deep in the familiar, forest time, and returning to the village, help me understand the many layers in my own life and the lives of women past and present."

Part I, "The Learner's Flame," reminds us that our "student" is always present and her creative fire needs tending throughout our lives. It is essential to devote attention to the flame of our true being and our creative nature, to discover practices that foster our inner life while being responsible in our relationships and work.

Part II, "The Householder," explores spiritual practices which bring balance to our life of work, family and community by applying the Benedictine way.

Part III, "Time in the Forest," addresses the longing for solitude that can lead us to seek time apart. There are many different paths into the forest and diverse experiences that surround solitude. Some of them are explored in this section and draw on the experiences of a variety of women.

Part IV speaks to the need to "Return to the Village" replenished from our forest time in order to participate in our daily life in ways that are more authentic to us and to our community.

Each rhythm contributes to a dynamic, ever-changing form of balance that is unique to each person. When we consciously choose to be aware of this balancing process, we will discover spiritual practices that support us as we travel our path.

We do not journey alone. We discover companions as we share our experience. This book provides an opportunity to walk with others. For example, recently a small group gathered in our living room. On that particular Saturday morning, we were exploring ways in which we can support the contemplative within each of us. I looked up the word "contemplative," which at its root means being with sacred space. As we explored this idea, one woman said: "There is such a longing for sacred space, space that allows me to go more deeply."

We can create this kind of environment for each other by setting time aside to share our experiences and support one another as we listen to our longings. *Deep in the Familiar* can be used by a group of women as a stimulus for personal reflection and discussion. It also encourages women to seek time apart when we can open ourselves to touch and be touched by the sacred in solitude. Whether you read this with others or on your own, it is my hope that this book will support and encourage you to explore the contemplative within yourself.

Reflection through a Journey Picture Exercise

Objective: To help you clarify where you are on your journey right now.

Time: Thirty to forty-five minutes or as long as it takes.

Materials needed: Large newsprint folded into four quadrants; colored markers/crayons.

Procedure: Use color, drawings, symbols, or collage (any way of expression except words) to respond to the following questions for reflection. Put your response to the question in the quadrant of your paper identified by the same number.

I	II
III	**IV**

   I. Where are you in your life journey right now?

  II. Where would you like to be?

 III. What is in your way, blocking you, keeping you from getting where you would like to be?

 IV. What would help you to get to where you want to be? What resources do you need to assist you?

It is helpful to reflect on the questions and then do this exercise in one sitting, but that is not necessary.

Suggestion

Hang your journey picture in a place where you can see it or, if you want to keep it private, take time to look at all four quadrants at once. Notice color, shape, themes that may go from quadrant to quadrant. Give it time to make its meaning known to you. Be open to it. Use your journal to record your awareness.

AT THE MONASTERY

Today I return to Transfiguration Monastery for what has become a yearly pilgrimage. This connection began three years ago when my husband and I were given time away, a sabbatical of five weeks. We chose to spend time in three different places where the contemplative life was honored and lived out. This Camoldolese Benedictine women's community was our first destination. I packed one of my bags full of manuscript pages, folders, old journals, and yellow legal pads. Just before we departed I decided to leave all that behind, to go with no agenda other than to replenish my soul.

I have come once again for that purpose now. Benedictine spirituality has been drawing me ever since my first visit to this monastery. Nuns and monks in this particular Benedictine order are called to live out a balanced life of community and solitude. This rhythm of time together and time apart supports me. I want to rest in it. I have come to the monastery as a learner to live for five days in that balance.

Sister Donald Corcoran, prioress of this community and a theologian engaged in East/West dialogue, speaks of the Benedictine Way as one of the great "schools for the education of the heart. ... Balanced, humane, yet challenging, it calls us to return again and again to the Center of all centers, not to exclude but to integrate."[3] It is to this place of learning that I return. I want to be open to what will happen in these days framed by the rhythm of communal prayer four times a day, periods of work and study, and the prevailing silence.

Soon after I arrive, I have tea with my friend who is the sister in charge of guests. I ask her what work I might do.

"What I need most," she says, "is someone to tend the wood-burning furnace in the guest house." How perfect to be asked to tend the flame for five days.

The commitment to keep the fire going becomes my focal point. I plan my activity and my rest in relation to it. The large, three-door furnace on the ground floor of the guest house becomes the center of my daily and nighttime life; the fueling ritual becomes an enactment of my need to concentrate on the fire within my being. Tending a fire takes concentration. The verb "to concentrate" comes from the Latin root which means to be with (con) the center (centrum). I need to bring my attention to the center, the heart of things, the furnace in this case, so that I can do the job that supports the community's ministry of hospitality.

There are several steps. When I enter the furnace room I have to close the door which usually stays open to circulate the heat more effectively. I do this so that smoke from the fueling process will not travel upstairs. Next, I open the window, so the smoke will be drawn out that way. Then I open the lowest iron door for circulation before opening the center door, which reveals the state of the fire. Smoke billows out; some seasoned kindling is needed. Coals glow; it is time to add some logs. Sister Jeanne-Marie says, "Logs are like people, they need to touch." And one night, after sleeping through the late watch, I find gray ashes with only a few remaining embers—just enough to begin again.

I learned years ago as an early childhood educator that a child's work is her play. Here my work has become my play. My focus is simply to keep the fire going. There is great enjoyment in the challenge. During these days, instead of writing, I am re-connecting with the qualities of the early learner inside of me. I slowly reclaim the joy that accompanies being fully engaged in learning. I feel the learner's fire rekindling in me.

After a few days of the Benedictine rhythm of prayer and work, I feel ready for the third component of life here: study. I am now available to be filled: to read or to listen to an occasional tape or to have an hour of conversation with one of the sisters. I am open to being fueled again with material that I can take into myself and consume for new forms of energy. Some material feels green and not right at first. When I take too much in, I feel overwhelmed.

One night when I wake at 1:30 A.M. to stoke the furnace, I return to bed realizing I can read as long as I want. In my single room I will not disturb anyone. I will not be sleep-deprived the following day because I can nap. What a joy! To my surprise, the same material that I had tried to read earlier leaps off the page and kindles all kinds of sparks in me. I feel clear and clean in my desire to continue. The material is just right. Like a child led by her play, I read and read until sleep finally takes over—amazed in the morning to find how much I retained from that nighttime of sheer delight!

Reflection

1. What gives you delight?
2. What ignites the spark of life in you?

3

THE LEARNER'S FIRE

The learner is alive and well inside each of us.

We come into the world as learners entering from the mystery of oneness, our first home. We begin life outside our mother's womb with a body memory of that primal experience. Then, in the early months of mother/child interdependency, we begin to learn as a "being-in-relation"[4] through our bodily needs. The newly born infant lies in the crook of the mother's arm, nestled against the curve of her breast. The baby sleeps while the mother waits, resting until the need of the little one leads the child to her mother's full breast.

We first recognize the familiar through smell. Very soon our other senses are available to us for our first learnings. We begin to slowly explore the world of our immediate experience: the body of our mother or father as they hold us, later our own bodies, and then a toy that comes within our grasp. We find different ways to relate to the object: We smell it, hear it, mouth it, see it, touch it. We wake up to our world through our senses. Memory is stored through this physical way of knowing. It is an essential part of our learning process.

Soon we begin to explore by moving out into the world of our immediate environment with encouragement and support from those who care for us. The rhythm is one of venturing and then returning to comfort and embrace. The "cruiser" learns to move along from couch to table leg to parent's leg in random fashion, until one day she fixes her eyes on an object with the intention of reaching it. This time she travels mindfully, guided by that focus. The ability to hold an intention and move toward a goal is at the core of the learner in each of us.

The world opens up for us as we move on our own and explore our surroundings. Everything is there waiting to be discovered. Going down the street on his mother's shoulders, a young child shouts: "Bird! House! Tree!" Awakened to all that is there, he begins to have words to name and claim his connection with the world outside himself. This is the child of delight alive with awareness and excitement.

We grow in our ability to attend to this world. We become able to approach something that we have not done before and we try it. Absorbed by the challenge, we repeat a motion, a sequence, an action over and over until we know how to do it. A child takes apart the works of a mini-flashlight. Through trial and error over a fifteen-minute period, she perseveres until she has put the parts back together and the light shines. Then, with continued absorption, she empties out the contents and repeats the process again and again.

At three and four years of age, we are natural explorers of our world. We grow by being drawn from safety toward delight. Abraham Maslow named these as the opposite poles on the spectrum of growth and learning. The pull toward delight seems to be innate for all of us, as is the pull toward safety.

The child of delight is present somewhere within each of us. As a learner in touch with her wholeness, she draws on all modes of perception: sensation, intellect, feeling, and intuition. Often we lose touch with this creative way of learning as we become task-oriented adults and limit ourselves to one expedient mode, forgetting how to explore with our whole self. We need to allow time to follow what is play for us. At the monastery I savored the freedom to follow my delight in reading without regard for the clock or the next day's appointments. When we take time for playful exploration, we add to our wholeness and health.

Play is not focused on a product but is a process. When I *do* my beach walk—agenda: twenty minutes of exercise—I am focused on producing a result: an aerobic workout. When I walk the beach—to just be there—I enjoy the whole process as it unfolds. I feel the water, smell the air. I see the patterns in the sand and explore the day's tidal offerings. When I delight in being caught up in that which presents itself in the moment, I am in sacred space. This can happen in any place, at any time, and at any age.

In those holy moments, we experience an openness within ourselves. This quality of availability is developed through most spiritual practices. To learn practices that support our continued growth and development, we can draw on the gifts from our early years: our connection with oneness and our interdependence, our body awareness, and our ability to stay with a focus and to persevere. These abilities enable us to tend the flame of our created nature as sacred mystery.

Tending the flame describes what we do in spiritual practice. The qualities that support our practice originate in our oneness with the creative fire of God, Divine Mystery. We can see these qualities so clearly in a young child, but forget that we have the same abilities. The complexity of adult life pulls us in so many directions through work, relationships, and all the attendant demands of the householding years. Anne Morrow Lindbergh named the power of that pull years ago in *Gift from the Sea*, when she spoke of the "centrifugal forces" that tend to pull us off center. We have the qualities within that can bring us back to the center. We can choose to recover them to support us in this intention. And when we get distracted, lose heart, or fall away, we can always begin again.

As a young mother, public school teacher, and minister's wife, I would often say to myself, "If only I were a nun . . . " I can recall the longing that accompanied those wistful words that meant: if I could just give myself to one thing, one focus, and go with it— give all my energy to it—then . . . At the time I never finished the sentence. The words drifted off into a longing, which I was at least naming. Perhaps my fantasy was this: If I were a nun, then . . . I could feel a sense of accomplishment, then . . . I could give myself to one thing and at the end of the day feel satisfied and maybe even complete.

I grew up as a Protestant in a Midwestern town during the forties and the fifties. I did not know anything about monastic life. What I did know was that nuns taught in the big Catholic school and that they wore black and white. Movies like *Going My Way* portrayed nuns living what appeared to be a focused life. My yearning later as a young mother was for a more centered way of living. There were intimations then of my need to make choices from the core of my being as I responded to the various components of my life as a householder; to find practices that kept me connected to the flame of my true being, my center.

I have come to trust and encourage others to listen to phrases like "If only I were . . . If only I could . . . If only there were a way to . . . " I believe these words often hold a spark of truth that deserves attention. When we take time to discover the truth beneath the words, we fan the coals of the sacred fire within.

In those early years of discovering how to be a mother of three young children, I did find ways to give myself to a single project or one idea for a period of time. One winter I made banners for everyone and every occasion. After the children went to bed, I used all the empty floor space to work or, more truly, play with my creations. Another year I made plastic flowers in the basement; another, I baked bread. Each required that I claim time to tend the creative fire within. I have found that when I do not allow some time for this expression, the untended fire can burn itself out. A fire that is tended over time burns long and continues to provide energy while we do other things.

Many of us have longings. "If only I could..." sounds within us. So often in our busy lives we store those yearnings away with a "someday" or a "maybe." It is important to find ways to bring these longings to the central hearth of our being as fuel for the expression of our created and creative nature. When we take time to hear the longing of our core being and give space in our life to express our yearnings, in whatever way we can manage, we are engaged in a practice which honors the sacred mystery that we are.

Reflection

1. Are you in touch with a longing at this time in your life?
2. Can you name it?

MY SOUL ENTIRE

Our first mode for learning is our body. As adults we find ourselves frequently disconnected from this original source of learning, our body—that grounded and intimate place of knowing. The sacred mystery of our body is as close to us as our breath, yet it is often the last place that we turn to as a source of wisdom.

My body recently claimed my attention. A flare-up came from within. It began at my center following the nerve that runs from my navel around my waist to my spine. It was shingles, which demanded immediate action: a new and expensive medication and a homeopathic remedy to try to prevent post-herpetic neuralgia. The first week all I could do was focus on the physical needs of my hurting body. Then I began to connect with emotions that were coming to the surface. I used my journal to do this. A review of the last two month's entries showed a recurring theme: I was exhausted.

I finally decided to dialogue with my body, a journal practice that has always engaged my body's innate wisdom. As adults we can draw on the knowing of our bodies, the kind of knowledge that we developed as young children. This "primordial sense of guidance" is available to us, according to Ira Progoff, creator of the Intensive Journal workshop. Through dialogue we can access "its natural wisdom" and apply it to our lives.[5]

Sometimes I address a part of my body, seeking its wisdom for me, like my aching back or throbbing head. In this case I engage my whole body in a dialogue which is written much like a theater script. I trust what comes and do not stop myself by thinking about the words.

JOAN: I realize how out of touch I have been. So much going on. . . . What are you trying to say to me?

BODY: I'm really sorry about what's happened. I hope the medication will do it and that your vigilance caught the shingles early enough.

JOAN: You were the one who got my attention.

BODY: I know. It's the only way I seem to be able to communicate with you. The subtle stuff doesn't work.

JOAN: I am discouraged. I thought I was better at handling stress.

BODY: Go easy, Joanie, now is not a time for recrimination. This is what's so and you need to work with that.

JOAN: We'll have to work together. You certainly can give clear signals.

BODY: And I will keep on doing it.

I continue the dialogue until it feels complete.

In that exchange, I heard my body's wisdom. It is true that when I feel vulnerable I often berate myself with judgments: How could you let this happen, you, who talk of self-care to others; you, who write about spiritual practice? I could feel the judging parts of me entering the scene like the biblical "friends" of Job, who offered "help" in his affliction, words which actually sound more like accusation and blame: What did you do to deserve this?

In contrast to my inner dialogue, a true friend spoke to me about how well I was tending myself in the middle of all this. I welcomed his words meant for the here and now in the midst of the pain. Encouragement was what I needed. It helped me recognize that this was an opportunity to learn more about tending the flame of my body.

When I "listened" to my body, I found that I wanted to walk in the early morning before others were up. It felt very healing for me to move and be alone in the outdoors. My early morning walk has always been a time for solitude. I realize now that this morning ritual has also been part of my spiritual practice.

To include our bodies in our spiritual practice may be confusing for some of us who come from a Judeo-Christian heritage that has often taught the separation of body and spirit. Within this tradition, for example, women's bodily rhythm of menstrual blood has been seen as a contamination of the sacred. In some places, the sacrament of communion was refused to menstruating women. A hierarchy of values placed the body at the base of the ladder that ascended toward the spiritual realm.

Our Puritan forebears in New England took this to the extreme and polarized body and spirit. Our cultural memory still retains the split. Even when we intellectually have challenged these religious and cultural beliefs and recognize the connection between body and spirit in our own experience, our early training may create remnants of resistance. For this reason I rejoice in and claim the heritage of Celtic Christian roots that abide in the deep soil of oneness.

The Celts lived on the islands of Britain and Ireland for centuries before the Anglo-Saxons. They experienced the sacred in the natural and material world and passed this rich heritage on through an oral tradition which shaped the prayers and blessings of the early Christians in those areas.

Celtic Christians followed the natural rhythms of the seasons. In fishing and farming, their work gave form to their days. The sacred and the ordinary were all of one piece, woven together through the events of daily life. The work of one's hands was sacred. This is so clear in the loom blessing. As a woman began weaving cloth for her household, she would offer these words:

> My warp shall be very even
> Give me thy blessing O God,
> And to all who are beneath my roof
> In the dwelling.[6]

Children said their morning prayers to the God of creation while they dressed or went to the "backhouse." All places were holy. Their words of praise, in what we would call the outhouse, expressed their embrace of body and spirit as one in God's presence. There was no hierarchy of value. An expression of the unity of all comes to us through one man's simple prayer, which he offered as he began his day: "Oh bless my soul entire."[7]

Spiritual practice depends on this unity and sense of wholeness beginning with our body, the vessel of our "soul entire." I doubt that Celtic Christians would even make the distinction to speak of "spiritual" practice. There was no separate category. Movement throughout the day was within the presence of the holy. Within this context, I will use the phrase "tending the flame" to include the practice of devotion to the sacredness of our soul entire.

My morning walk is part of my practice. As I walk, I feel my kinship with the Celtic people who journeyed daily from place to place. As they walked to the fields or to the village, they offered prayers that connected their body's motion with the movement of

God's purpose for their lives. This simple, ancient journey prayer often sounds within me as I match my step to the rhythm of the words and repeat them as I walk.

> I on thy path, O God.
> Thou, O God, in my steps.[8]

This morning I have two possible routes before me: one to the beach and one to the cemetery. I turn them over in my mind. Today I am clear that I need solitude.

It is very early. Quiet. My feet hit the pavement, solitary sounds as I set out. I let my body feel the day and awaken to the brushing mist as I move purposefully up School Street toward Beech Grove Cemetery. Memories of my body's immobility, days on my back and other periods of limitation, merge with gratitude, for I am aware of the support of my legs. It is good to move freely again—to breathe deeply as I enter the cemetery by the road that winds up the hill. Crows caw, their familiar cry rebounds off granite gravestones. The sound, softened by ancient trees, is welcoming.

I breathe deeply again. In this place I can just be. I don't have to engage in conversation. I can open myself to the present by being in the midst of the past. Thoughts come and go as my feet follow the small roads that wind back and forth between the family plots. When I come to this place, I go beyond day-to-day complexity and concerns.

I am aware of time passing, life and death, as I read the headstones simply saying: Mother, Daughter, Devoted wife of . . . , infant child; Our Eve—age 6 years 1 month. The family names are well known to me after twenty-three years in this New England town. People who were here when we arrived, no longer are living. I remember them as I pass their stones. In my years of returning to this place, I have noted the way the cemetery has always been well kept and obviously tended.

Our gravesite is here. We have the certificate from the Department of Public Works that records the sale of our particular plot of ground, "including perpetual care." I recall the last words of Friedrich von Hügel: "Caring is the greatest thing, caring matters most." They still speak to me. Yet it is this caring that often gets me overinvolved, overcommitted, overtired—to the point of driving myself beyond what my body can sustain—and my health usually breaks down.

It is actually the "forever" that I come to touch here in this cemetery. I come to gain perspective on the immediate concerns of my life. Being here is like wearing bifocals for me. I need both lenses to see my life more clearly: one to see the things that are right before me and one for a greater, wider, and larger view. This ritual of returning is purposeful. I need what I call the perspective of eternity that can be summed up in the paradox: Everything matters and nothing matters.

Memories come to the surface of my consciousness as I walk here. Stored mysteriously in my body, they rise from the depths of my life experience to join in this moment as I seek to gain perspective. Memory, says John O'Donohue, is "a kind of awakening and integrating of everything that happens to you. It is part of the process of reflection which gives great depth to experience."[9]

On a familiar path, I recall other times that I have actively sought this perspective of eternity. I remember coming to this place a few days after returning from our sabbatical, that gift of time several years ago. In the first days back, everything seemed to crowd in on me. I felt overwhelmed. I came here early one morning to regain the long-distance perspective as I faced choices that were before me. I walked through the old cemetery to the new section, less familiar to me.

My eyes were drawn to a woman's gravestone. Her dates shouted at me: 1938, my birth year, to 1993. I stopped short. She is no longer living and I am alive! I slowed my pace, deeply affected by that reality. It was good to be reminded once again of the simple gift of life itself. As I rounded a bend in the road, I was drawn to notice another stone. It was the name engraved upon the granite that leaped out at me: DRIVER.

The driver in me responded immediately. It is the familiar part of me that pushes. My driver is the one that operates from the belief that it's never enough, I am not enough... there is always more I can do. I had been feeling that driver energy, the pushing energy, activated once again by our return to town—the place of community, family, and work.

Another memory comes, a time when I was unable to *do* anything. I was a spectator and observer of life, sleeping and spending my days on the living room floor because of a back injury. I awoke one morning to the sounds of others in the house rising, getting ready to go to school and work, eating breakfast, and then walking past the closed living room door as they left the house for the day. Each was caught up in living his or her own life. And I lay there, observing from the vantage point of what felt like eternity. I watched from another dimension as life went on... without me.

As I remember that time when life did go on without me, my present focus broadens. I begin to let in the larger dimension of continuous life, trend, history, era, eons of time. I recall the ancient glacier at Mount Rainier slowly melting over millions of years, drop by drop. I touch the mystery of creation and my small part in it. I turn to phrases from Psalm 8 that I have adapted and made my own.

When I consider the heavens, the works of your hands...
Who are we that you are mindful of us and our children
    that you care for us?...
Yet you have made us little lower than the angels...
You have crowned us with glory and honor...
You have made us one with all creation.

Time stands still. This divine "caring forever" breaks through and for that moment shatters the bonds that I have created in my struggle and strain over life's complexities. I am freed to go to the still, quiet place where the Holy One touches me in my soul and we are one for moments and all else falls away.

When I finally turn to leave, words come from within: Tend the flame *now*. You are part of the creative fire of God. Listen to your body. Stay with what is before you right now. Walk your path, step-by-step. Let the flame lead you.

On my way home I pass familiar houses and gardens. As the church bell rings seven times, my eyes rise to the steeple, landmark of our town, known for years as the "Old Sloop" to fishermen, guiding them as they have headed home. For me, as a minister's wife, child, and grandchild, it is a personal symbol. The towering white steeple often dominates the scene.

This morning, however, as I approach both church and parsonage, my eye is drawn to a window in our living room. Within I see a single candle flame, signaling to me that my husband is still meditating. I stop outside for a moment to view both the steeple and the flame. It is the quiet flame that draws me, the promise of silence within that brings me home.

Reflection Following a Dialogue with Your Body

Objective: To access the wisdom of your body.

Time: Thirty minutes.

Materials needed: Journal; a quiet space to relax.

Procedure:

Preparation: Lie down for relaxation or sit in a comfortable and quiet place. Keep your journal and pen nearby. Begin with some deep breathing; let your body be supported and rest in that support. Then return to your own natural rhythm of breathing.

Relaxation: Bring your attention to your head and be aware if there is any tension in your forehead, eyes, etc. Move your attention slowly, scanning your body in this fashion. Be aware that if there is tension in a part of your body, it may want your further attention. Just notice and pass down your body all the way to your toes.

Dialogue: Let your awareness return to the place in your body that most needs or calls for your attention. As you feel ready, turn to your journal and begin writing a dialogue with that part. Address it by name with a question and write out the dialogue that follows. Bring the conversation to an end by thanking your body and acknowledging that you can continue your dialogue as needed.

An example of a dialogue:

JOAN: Gut, why are you clutching in this safe place?

GUT: I'm clutching because you are pushing on yourself to get this written.

JOAN: (I take a deep sigh.) I *have* to get this done, the group starts Tuesday. I'm still writing material.

GUT: Did you notice how you relaxed me when you let go into that sigh. I liked that, it felt real good.

JOAN: Yes, I did notice.

GUT: Well, try it again.

I do, continuing the dialogue until it feels complete.

Instruction: Play with your dialogue.

Reflection after the Dialogue

1. What wisdom does your body have for you right now?

2. In what ways do you feel called to attend to your body?

5

FEMININE FOCUS

Our living room has *shibumi*. I was introduced to this wonderful word she-boo-me by a Japanese Dominican priest. He referred to an object or space as having the quality of shibumi when it has been used countless times for sacred purposes, as a Japanese tea bowl or a bench in an old Quaker meeting house worn smooth from years of use. We sense *shibumi* in this space, so much living has happened here.

This room has been the gathering place of a New England parsonage since 1830. Over the years it has been used for baptisms, weddings, and funerals. During the past twenty-three years of our tenure, it has provided space for rich life. It is where we meditate morning and evening. When our children were young, we created a birthday ritual of "hunt and find" that took place here. Brother and sisters hid the presents. Then the person of the day searched for them, responding to clues of "colder, cooler, warmer, hot, hotter!" shouted by the family.

I slept on this floor for fourteen days when I could barely move from a back injury. Years ago our children put on an autumn picnic for us in this room, leaves and all. Groups meet here. My work with women began within these walls when together we discovered the deep well of our shared experience and continued to meet to encourage each other in our individual journeys. Other groups gather here: some for sharing, some for planning, and some for meditation.

We walk in this room as a form of meditation, slow walk, as it is called in Zen practice. This has been a healing practice for me. It slows me down, giving my body a chance to move at one with the rhythm of my breath. At times when I need focus, I use a breath phrase, repetitive words that reach my soul: "I in Thee and Thou in me," repeated in rhythm with my in-breath and out-breath as my slow steps follow the edge of our green rug.

There was a time when I was so consumed with anger that I felt captive to it, holding on to my righteousness. I could not let it go. To forgive felt beyond me, and yet I knew it was the only way to freedom within. And so I walked, several times a day, around the rug. Slow walk, step-by-step, repeating in rhythm the words: "Healing and forgiving love. Healing and forgiving love," over and over, day after day, month after month, until I felt a slow release of my inner clenched hand. I finally walked into an opening, a letting go—my way into grace and the gift of forgiving love. The memory and sense of that powerful experience comes back to me as I move in this space.

I meet with individual women in this living room. The shared learning moves back and forth between us like the rhythm of my rocking chair, the same chair in which I held an infant grand-daughter, trying to rock away the pain of her ear infection. In this same chair I have also rocked my own inner child in times of pain.

Today I sit across from a woman who directs a human service agency in our community. Her work is challenging, often painful, yet she provides creative and caring leadership. As a wife and mother of two young people, her caregiving energy is in great demand. In addition, her mother was dying of cancer and she had

come to live with the family. The daughter's days now included
managing the twenty-four-hour care of her mother.

At this point, the woman described herself as an elastic band
that was stretched and pulled in so many directions that she felt
frayed. "I've never experienced so much stress in my life. I *have*
to draw on my deepest resources to make it through day by day."
This woman returned to counseling to commit herself to tend the
flame of her true being in the midst of such demands.

She was clear about her needs. "I have got to take care of
myself. I am walking each morning and that is so good. But I have
not been able to write in my journal or to meditate. The room
where we meditate is now the bedroom for the person who lives
with us to help with my mother." We talked about space and we
talked about her daily schedule. Her motivation to make changes
was high, for her need was great. "If I could make a transition time
between work and home and find space to meditate, that would
be a beginning." She decided to speak with a neighbor who has
been offering her space "for the last twenty years," and she smiled
as she realized that it had taken this level of stress for her to
respond to that offer. "I could walk to her place, spend twenty
minutes meditating, and walk home." Her first step was to talk
with her friend.

She never got to do that. Her mother's condition intensified
and she died within the week. The daughter's exhaustion, grief
for her mother, and the pain in her daily work all are contributing
to increased feelings of stress. Like many of us, she is tempted to
lose herself in activity and has to make some conscious choices:
"I need to meditate. I am not taking care of myself!" This time we
talk about carving out a small space in her house, using a prayer
bench and a simple altar in the corner of a room. We agree that
it is necessary to be very practical when we are tending the flame.

We often literally have to make space in our lives in an external way in order to focus and clear the internal space.

Each of us has life situations that confront us and often force us to draw more deeply on our resources. These circumstances challenge us to discover or return to practices that spiritually support us in hard times. As difficult as our situation may be, it presents opportunities to learn ways or practices that deepen our union with God in the midst of our circumstances.

Not long ago I sat in my rocking chair across from a woman whose work in a helping profession also brought her to the need for time apart to reflect on her life. Our sessions provided support for her exploration. She spoke of her need for focus in this way:

> I get this image of a container that has too many holes within. Things are moving through it too fast. There is not enough containing going on. That's what it is like for me right now. Things come in and go out, without my being able to absorb them, really take them in and assimilate them into my whole system. I need a spiritual practice that will help me to close those holes so that things can come and go but I can take them in more fully. A daily meditation practice would make a real difference.

Her words moved me. In a deeply feminine way she had described a longing for focus and the need for a form of meditation practice. In expressing her need for a space within which lets things come in and out, absorbing and assimilating what will nurture and feed life, she used a womb-centered way of describing meditation practice.

Her image evoked body memories of a time when a womb-centered rhythm was very physical for me. With pregnancy my energy would often feel drawn into that center place within me and all else would fade. At other times I would actually feel my energy moving out from my womb, generating care and nurturing energy to those relationships that were part of my daily life. That physical awareness of my center helped create a more balanced rhythm between inner and outer movement during those gestation months for me.

I also have a body memory of that final stage of pregnancy where everything comes together in the power of the push. Recently I have watched each of my daughters push her firstborn child down the birth canal and into life outside the womb.

all focus

all purpose

all being

Oned

into

that

moment

to bring

forth

life!

There are moments in our lives as women when we know this kind of intensely focused, burning energy that is essential to the act of birthing and creation. There seems to be a balancing rhythm unique to each of us that moves from the focus of containing and gestation to the focus of the creative push. To find our own unique balance with these two kinds of foci is essential to the well-being of our soul entire. It often involves finding the balance, losing it, and refinding it.

When I am writing and have momentum, I feel the urge to push: There is so little time! I want to get this completed! It is often premature, and at those moments I am grateful for Thomas Merton's words, which I keep on my desk.

> At the moment, the writing is one thing that gives me access to some real silence and solitude. Also I find that it helps me to pray because when I pause at my work I find that the mirror inside me is surprisingly clean and deep and serene and God shines there and is immediately found, without hunting.[10]

I need the reminder of an open and receptive focus. Yet I live and work in my home and am connected to others' lives. So when I have writing time, I often feel an urgency to produce. How can I keep the momentum of my writing and at the same time be open to the interactions of my life as a householder? Can I trust that the "interruptions" of my relationships may actually add to the substance of my writing?

The time set aside for writing becomes an opportunity to confront the driver in me and to learn more about my need to feel in control. I am challenged to trust the feminine way of focusing, which includes both the creative push and my availability to life's coming and goings. I draw on my daily meditation practice to teach me how to be an open space that can hold, absorb, and assimilate as well as let the waters of life move on through. The impact of this practice is gentle and subtle. I speak as a beginner, an early learner who falls and gets up, topples and tumbles, moves forward and sideways in order to gain momentum for a more balanced life walk.

I have had many teachers over the years. My introduction to meditation came through my husband. As a minister's daughter and granddaughter, I swore that I would never marry a minister. However, I fell in love with a man who grew up in Quaker meetings where silence leads and there are no ordained clergy. He was later led by the inner light to seminary and eventually to the Protestant church. His journey continues to be a profound and unique route within Protestantism. His presence in my life has touched depths that I never imagined could be there. We share the love of silence.

Cam's own journey of faithfulness to his nature, heritage, and contemplative calling has been a steady witness. I remember the early years. I can see him now sitting in our bedroom in meditation posture with at least one small child on his lap. His door was open and his concentration was strong. It was a welcoming space for our children. It was, however, threatening to me at first. Somehow I feared this practice was taking him away from me. I did not know then that being faithful to his spiritual practice would enable him to be more fully himself in the midst of all the demands of his life and in our marriage.

Until recently, the way of the contemplative has often been a lonely walk within the Protestant church. My husband's perseverance has encouraged me to find my own way into a practice of meditation. Like the women who share their journeys with me, I feel an urgent need to be faithful to my practice as I walk through my days step-by-step. For me it is one way to come home to my true being and to deepen my union with God.

Reflection

1. What in your life right now is challenging you to draw on resources that deepen your spiritual life?

2. What practices help you to keep your focus when you feel challenged or pulled off balance?

6

BE AWAKE!

There is an ancient story which tells of a learner who came to the teacher and asked, "Is there anything I can do to make myself enlightened?" The teacher responded, "As little as you can do to make the sun rise in the morning."

"Then of what use," exclaimed the learner, "are the spiritual exercises that you have given me?"

"To make sure," the teacher said, "that you are not asleep when the sun begins to rise."[11]

We can begin by being awake to the present moment. Our breath can lead us there. When we emerge from sleep there is an instant when we sense that first shift in consciousness: We know that we have left the region of sleep and have just had a conscious thought. From that point on we can choose to notice our breath and use it to help us to become more fully present in our daily life. Thich Nhat Hanh, a Vietnamese Buddhist monk who worked within his war-torn country as a force for reconciliation for many years, speaks clearly as a teacher of this way into mindfulness.

Breathing in and out is very important, and it is enjoyable. Our breathing is the link between our body and our mind. Sometimes our mind is thinking one thing and our body is

doing another, and mind and body are not unified. By con-
centrating on our breathing, "In" and "Out," we bring body
and mind back together, and become whole again... when
we breathe consciously we recover ourselves completely and
encounter life in the present moment.[12]

The practice of following our breath can be done anywhere:
driving on the freeway, peeling vegetables, waiting on a customer,
tending a toddler, chairing a board meeting, listening to another's
pain, changing a tire, or approaching a difficult person. The miracle of our breath is that it is always available to re-mind us, to
bring the mind back to what is before us in the present moment.

Wisdom often lies below the surface of our common phrases.
"I'll be back as soon as I can, but don't hold your breath." Conscious breathing in times of waiting is a choice we can make to
enable us to be present whether we are waiting in line for a gro-
cery check-out or waiting for a doctor's call. Waiting in the "place
of not knowing" can be the most difficult place for us. We wait
for the safe arrival of a loved one or to be told by a doctor what
we do not want to hear. This is often a time of mental agitation.
Our minds search for explanations, causes, meaning, anything to
hold on to in the midst of a tossing sea of uncertainty. It is very
difficult to resist anxious churning while waiting. It is, however,
possible to give our mind and heart something else on which to
focus as a way to move through these times of not knowing. Our
breath can assist us.

The natural pace of our in-breath and out-breath can slow our
racing minds. A simple exercise can be done in a waiting room
or anywhere that we can close our eyes and use our imagination.
Breathe in a calming color; for me, sea green has a healing effect.
Imagine the color filling your body; then breathe out another

color, like smoky gray, which might represent tension and worries: What if the doctor finds a mass? What if my son didn't get that job? Extend the exhale before filling your lungs again, imagining the air as a color that is healing or calming for you. After using this breathing exercise for several minutes, we can choose to turn our focus to an external object: a statue in the waiting room or a tree outside the window. At this point, we need to consciously choose to observe it with full attention, experiencing it with our senses like a young child who encounters an object for the first time. While we concentrate in this way, our breath can support our intention when unbidden thoughts or feelings come. We can be aware without judgment of thoughts and feelings that go through our minds, allow them to move through, and then gently re-turn our attention to the object.

The practice of letting thoughts and feelings come and go is very different from repressing or pushing away what feels distracting or threatening. The energy that it takes for us to resist these thoughts and feelings is freed to engage actively in bringing ourselves back to the present. An aid to keeping the focus is to be conscious of our breath as a sensation moving through our nostrils. As I follow my breath into the center of my being, I become aware in my body that I can also open space for these thoughts and feelings to move on through. This womb-centered way to focus is different from the top-heavy, mental absorption that follows a thought or feeling down a maze and often corners it, only to get caught going in circles in that small space. Our breath provides an avenue into the practice of meditation.

There is no one right way to meditate. Each of us needs to discover what works best for us. There are many different forms of practice. Ultimately they all lead to an inner place of stillness.

At this time in my life, I set aside twenty minutes in the early morning for my practice. The following instructions present a way into meditation that I find very helpful:

Sit down. Sit still and upright. Keep your eyes slightly open, allowing your gaze to fall unfocused about three feet in front of you. Sit relaxed and alert.

Silently, within yourself begin to say a single word or phrase joined with your inhalation or exhalation or both.

Depending on your spiritual tradition or individual choice, the word can provide a focus and is most effective if its meaning does not engage your conscious mind. Select a word or phrase or, as is often the case, let the word select you.

Sound it gently but continuously in your heart, the center of your being, letting go of all thought of its meaning.

Do not imagine anything—spiritual or otherwise. When thoughts, feelings, and images come up, let them come and let them go. Just return again to simply saying the word or phrase in the depth of your being.[13]

Some days the thoughts and feelings dominate and it is very difficult to reach a place of stillness. At these times, it is reassuring to know that simply sitting for a short period of time, placing my body where my intention is, can be my practice for the day. There are also days when my focus is steadier and my mantra enables me to empty myself and I do become a receptive space for silence. The daily practice helps me to keep that space within open to the flow of the Spirit. It also makes me more aware and available to cooperate with intimations of the Spirit moving in my life throughout the day.

For my meditation time this summer morning, I sit on the porch of the homestead of my family. Down the hill from where I sit lies the large, oval-shaped conservation pond. It was built twenty-five years ago, the realization of my mother's dream of a place for children, grandchildren, and now great-grandchildren to swim. A fresh, cold, spring-fed mountain stream feeds the pond.

Earth moving equipment prepared the site for the pond, creating a dam and a rim to contain water that was diverted from the brook. An underground pipe runs down the hill from the brook to the excavated space, conveying the clear, cold water. The pond stays fresh because of an outflow pipe that pulls the water by gravity back out into the stream. The pond water then rejoins the brook in its journey toward the big river.

Today, as I look out to the pond, I am awake and very aware of my body as I sit erect on a chair with a cushion that tilts my pelvis. This has become a comfortable posture. I hold my hands in front of my belly, the left hand resting in the palm of my right hand with the tips of my thumbs lightly touching. The open space between fingers and thumb forms an oval facing out toward the pond. This position is restful. I follow my thoughts as they go to the pond.

The surface of the pond is still today, though fish and frogs dwell in it and a great blue heron occasionally visits its grassy edges. Humans plunge into its depth—often with shouts as every pore responds to the cold, cold freshness. "Be awake!" is the message from this living water. Can I let these thoughts go now, trusting that I will absorb their nourishment and then later put them down on paper? I allow them to go, letting my gaze fall to three feet in front of me. I return to my breath.

To bring myself back to my rhythm of breathing, a shorter inhale and a longer exhale, I imagine a waterfall pouring down a mountainside. As I exhale, I slowly let my breath fall out of me and I sense an emptying within. In yoga, this way of exhaling is called the Falling Away Breath. I begin to let go into the silence.

I gently move to one of the mantras that over time have come to me, connecting a seven-syllable word or phrase with my rhythm of inhaling and exhaling. "I in Thee and Thou in me" has become the main breath prayer that I use. I also find the Aramaic word "Maranatha" to be a helpful sound focus, because it does not engage my mind. According to biblical records, Jesus used the word. It means "Come, Lord," but my attention is not on the meaning, rather it is on the syllable sounds which help create an openness within: "Ma-ra-na-tha."[14]

On days when it is hard to focus and I am not sitting before a still pond but feel instead like I am caught in a sea squall, I count my breaths from one to ten. Inhaling "one," exhaling "one"; inhaling "two," exhaling "two," and so on. This helps me to simply keep my focus on my breath. When I am anxious, this conscious breathing is harder to do but all the more important. Fritz Perls, father of Gestalt psychology, claimed that anxiety is 90 percent due to a lack of oxygen. I am grateful to have learned deep breathing during childbirth. I draw on this kind of abdominal breathing when anxiety begins to rise. Once again I follow my breath to my center to slow me down and focus my attention there rather than in my head.

Several years ago, at a time of extreme anxiety when fears were racing through me, I came to the old cabin that stands beside the brook that feeds our pond. It was Memorial Day and time to open up for the season, to sweep out the nestings and droppings of the winter inhabitants. Often it is a place where I meditate, but that day I was too worn out to sit up. So I claimed my seasonal occupancy by resting on the bed in the corner. I lay there enveloped by the sound of the brook. I began to breathe more deeply. I took up my mantra, breathing in and out, one with the sound of the water. New lines added themselves to my breath prayer.

> I in Thee and Thou in me
> the sound of water flowing.
> I in Thee and Thou in me
> deeper than all knowing.

The words moved through me and I slowly let go into a level of resting that I had not known for weeks. To rest in the presence of the Holy One is one way to be awake to the present moment.

I find encouragement in the simple Rule of Taizé which is used by the Protestant monastic community in Taizé, France. In this brief book of instruction, the prior speaks about the Daily Office, that structure of corporate prayer that is central to their daily life and practice. "There will be days when the office is a burden to you. On such occasions know how to offer your body, since your presence already signifies your desire, momentarily unrealizable, to praise your Lord."[15] To put our body where our intention is and then to let go into rest can be a way to tend the flame.

Through mindful living, walking, and sitting meditation practice, we acknowledge sacred mystery—our own and the mystery of the Divine Presence. These practices are gentle. They cannot be rushed. They need to be done with the perseverance of an early learner who repeats over and over a newfound skill until it becomes part of him or her. Often there are not immediate results, but rather a subtle and gradual sense of movement, guidance, and balance in our daily lives.

We live our way into these practices. In so doing we honor the call to tend the flame. If we neglect the flame, we also cut ourselves off from the source of energy that is available to us when we are one with our deep self. To be awake to that calling we need to persevere with practices that breathe life into the flame that is uniquely ours.

The initial flame
ignites
then shrinks
My hand comes up
to assist
hurry it along
make it bigger
so I can see—now!
through this dim dawn
of early morning.

"Let it be"
rises
from deep inside me
and surely—
hand withdrawn
the flame
slowly
takes its shape
full
filling
this space
with
steady
quiet
light.

Reflection

1. How do you respond to silence?

2. Can you find ten to twenty minutes to meditate and be still? How do you do this? What resources do you draw on for this practice?

3. What helps you "stay awake" to the sacred in the moment?

Part
II

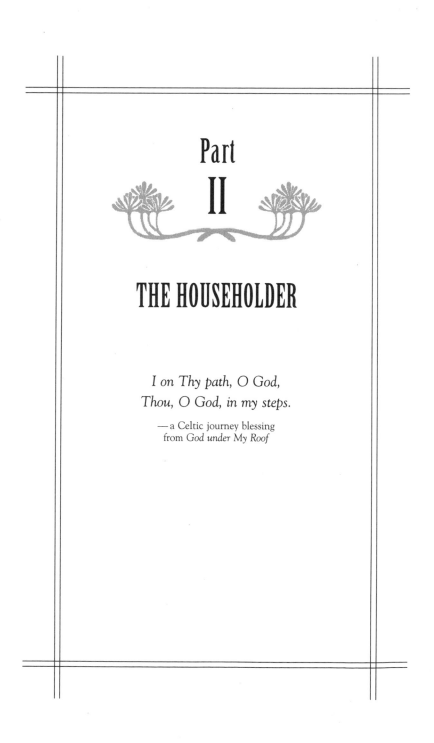

THE HOUSEHOLDER

I on Thy path, O God,
Thou, O God, in my steps.

—a Celtic journey blessing
from *God under My Roof*

A HOUSEHOLDER'S PRACTICE

The fifth-century Hindu life phase tradition originally described the experience of men in an Indian culture. The life stages began with the student years, followed by the householding years—those years during which a person established himself in the market place with work and in the village with family and community. However, time for replenishment of soul was also considered an essential part of the four stages of life. Therefore, when a man saw the sons of his sons, he left his family and possessions and went into the forest to live as a hermit. Through various spiritual practices and time for reflection during that forest time, he would attempt to come to the experience of mystical union and "enter the fourth and final stage of life, wandering the land, emancipated from all desire and suffering."[16]

This ancient tradition is now honored in some contemporary Indian families in which both men and women recognize their need for forest time. Their understanding of the last two life stages is closer to that of Edith Sullwold, master therapist and teacher in this country, who introduced me to forest time. It is a time for "assimilation, distillation and integration." Time in the forest enables a person to then return to the marketplace or village in order "to be there in a new way."[17]

Most of us entering the twenty-first century experience the more fluid nature of our life phases. We often find ourselves journeying alongside travelers of various ages, who traditionally would have belonged in different stages. Some people are falling in love and marrying or taking partners in their seventies. Others are having babies and establishing households in their forties after years in the marketplace. The years in the marketplace may be shortened due to downsizing or lengthened because of social security extension. Young people are experiencing loss through cancer, AIDS, and other diseases that bring them closer to their elders who are also facing their mortality directly.

Given this awareness of the fluid and unpredictable nature of contemporary life, it is essential to take time to reflect in the midst of our householding. Part II was written as a way to assimilate, distill, and integrate my own experience. These chapters are offered to stimulate reflection on your own familiar life of work, family, and community. The following journal exercise may help to begin that process.

Reflective/Receptive Journal Exercise

Objective: To reflect on your life as a householder.

Time: Thirty minutes.

Materials needed: Journal, pen or pencil, timer; quiet space.

1. What words or phrases describe your householding life right now? Make a list of words quickly on one page in your journal.

2. When you have finished that list, put your pen in your nondominant hand as a way to access your more intuitive side.

Then ask yourself: What quality do I most need to help me in my householding life at this time (for example: courage, flexibility, humor, etc.)? Close your eyes and be open to the word that draws you. When the word has chosen you, write it at the top of a clean journal page.

3. Take four minutes to brainstorm this word by listing associated words that come up when you focus on your word. Use your dominant hand in the list-making process. If your thoughts are off the wall, put them down. If you are stuck, repeat your original word. Keep going until the time is up.

4. Stop. Change your position, move around. Find a comfortable spot to relax. Keep your journal and pen near you. Close your eyes; follow your breath into relaxation. Open yourself in a receptive state, and then return to your word. Be with it as if you were holding it gently in open hands. When you are ready, use your nondominant hand to write whatever comes. You may feel slowed down and awkward. Take the time that you need. Trust your experience.

AT THE MUSEUM

In my late forties, I was at an impasse: struggling to make a hard decision regarding my work as a mental health counselor. I was wrestling with my options until I exhausted myself and developed laryngitis. I had to take time off from work. Months earlier I had reserved a ticket to the Museum of Fine Arts in Boston to see "Monet in the '90s: The Series Paintings." I had looked forward to going alone. As the time approached, I struggled as to whether I could make it. It seemed important to go.

Crowds were waiting at the door that morning. As a way to be alone with the paintings and to learn more about Monet, I rented a cassette player. The commentator's voice came through my headset as I moved into the exhibition room's rectangular space. My eyes were drawn to Monet's series of haystacks, this one subject, seen, known, painted over and over again. As I heard the commentator speak of Monet's purpose, letting nature be experienced through this one focus, I had a sense of the Eternal.

I walked from painting to painting, through the subtle changes in time of day and season reflected in those stacks of grain to which Monet returned again and again. Tears came as I connected with a profound longing in my heart to be so fully present. From somewhere within me I heard the words "going deep in the familiar." That was it. That was what Monet was doing. In that moment I connected with the power of that phrase. I also re-connected in memory with a time in my life when I knew that way of living through my own experience.

Many years before, when I was twenty-two and newly married, my husband and I had gone to Edinburgh for his last year of seminary. We anticipated being able to travel during the holidays, staying in youth hostels on the Continent. However, en route to Scotland we learned that I was pregnant. By holiday time, it was clear that extended travel was not advisable. Instead of discovering new countries and continents, we were to discover something else, something that Cam named: going deep in the familiar.

The limitations of my pregnancy became my field of practice for this exploration. I began to follow the changes in my body. Eventually I slowed down. My attention was being drawn to the sacred right here, now, in the place most intimate to me: my body. I became aware of opportunities for learning that came in the simple aspects of my life. The daily trips to the butcher, the fruitier, and the baker became a ritual of familiarity. As I walked back and forth, I *really* saw the daffodils pushing through the snow, and the roses . . . oh, the roses! All that once seemed ordinary and familiar became for me a way to touch the sacred.

As I look back now, I see what an unexpected gift that was. It provided me with an experience of going deep right in the midst of my everyday life to experience moments of oneness with creation, within me and around me. Thirty years later, my yearning for a deeper sense of my union with the Eternal was palpable as I heard the words sounding again within me . . . going deep in the familiar.

I came to the museum in the cold of winter, feeling as barren of possibility as the frozen ground that day. I left with the images of subtle changes that can be seen when one is focused and aware.

I rediscovered words that named for me my longing to be present now in my life in a different way. I returned home with a question.

How can I be receptive and available to be touched by the Eternal in the now of my life? I had asked this question and felt the longing beneath the question before. This time, however, my tears of recognition confirmed the truth of my need to stay with my longing and to see where it led me. Deep within myself, beneath my exhaustion, my questions, and my longing, I felt a response. It was a whole body/soul kind of Yes—a knowing—that quietly confirmed the importance of continuing this quest.

Reflection

Right now you may be fully engaged in relationships or situations that call upon you to be fully present right where you are. Can you take time to follow these suggestions?

1. Recall a moment in the midst of your daily life when you were fully present to your oneness with creation and/or the Eternal, a moment when you had a sense of that connection. Can you draw on your senses to describe that experience in your journal or relive it in your memory?

2. What touched you most deeply at that time?

THE LONGING

It was several years later and two nights before my husband and I were to depart for Transfiguration Monastery in Windsor, New York. For a brief time we were leaving our life as householders—established in our family, work, and community—and going on a sabbatical journey.

I had a dream that woke me: I had lost something of great importance to me and was desperately trying to find it. As I lay in bed with the anxiety from the dream still with me, I became conscious of my fear that in the midst of my busy life I might lose touch with my soul.

I recorded the dream and my feelings about it in my journal.

I CANNOT CAPITULATE to all the voices that pull me away. The longing to go deeper in the contemplative way has brought me to this point in the journey, *I will not abandon myself.*

Words of the psalmist then came to me.

> Like a deer yearns for the living water
> even so is my soul, O God. (Psalm 42:1)

I was longing to be in a place where the daily life was replenished by a rhythm of communal prayer and work, study, silence, and solitude.

When we finally arrived at the monastery, first stop on our five-week venture, our friend the guest mistress welcomed us warmly. She told us a little about this women's community that she and two other nuns founded twenty years ago. Then she instructed us in the ways of the guesthouse and the times of prayer that are called the Daily Office. My husband and I recognized that we each had different needs and wanted to respect those differences. We found the observance of silence in the house a welcome relief. We did not have to make conversation with the other guests or each other; we were free to stay with our own experience. We walked and talked outdoors whenever we wanted to do so. Sometimes at meals the guests joined each other to share experiences and the delicious food.

The simple chapel is part of a log building, warmed by powerful icons, candles, and the voices of the sisters as they pray the psalms, sing the responses, and listen to scripture and other sacred readings. As we joined them in morning prayer at 6:30 A.M., the noonday office, evening prayer, and finally Compline just before going to bed, I became aware that we were not saying or reading the psalms: We were praying them. I let the words wash over and through me, no longer trying to understand all the words. I began to feel the effects on me and was encouraged in my surrender by Thomas Merton who wrote about praying the psalms.

> Above all don't be worried about the pace, about what is happening or not happening, about what seems to be going on on the surface. Hand that over to God, and believe that below the surface your mind and will and heart are being drawn into a place where God is at work.[18]

Each morning until 9:30 there was individual quiet time for breakfast, prayer with spiritual reading, reflection, and study. Then work projects began. As I became more aware of the sisters throughout the day, I realized that these nuns worked very hard. I watched my friend in some of her many roles in this small community. As well as being guestmistress, she is the sacristan who prepares the chapel and takes the lead in the daily office of prayer. She also performs secretarial duties for the community.

I knew that hospitality is central to the Benedictine Way. In the guide that was written for all Benedictine communities, the monks are instructed: "Let everyone that comes be received as Christ." The Rule of Saint Benedict goes on to say that it is the leaders who are to show the community "the price and the process of availability and hospitality and presence to others."[19] It is a way of openness that I would love to feel generating from my own heart. This generosity of spirit is something that I have also seen in my own parents' lives. However, before I left home for this sabbatical time I felt fragmented by the many roles that I play. I had very little left in my reserve to reach out to others. I felt depleted and contracted in my heart.

I questioned my friend, whom I found involved in many of the same tasks that I have. "How do you *not* get pulled and pushed by all these aspects of your life?"

Her response was immediate: "It's the times of prayer—the Daily Office—then everything stops. That is what makes everything else possible." I lived with her clear answer and recorded my response in my journal.

I am finally getting it. I never "got it" before now. Everything comes out of prayer.

I want to learn from her way of being fully present to that which is before her. I want to know more about her vows and how they might help me in my life as a householder.

I began to feel the rhythm of their day. The pace itself was replenishing, this balanced way of prayer, work, and study. I changed my way of study. "Read little, ponder much" is the advice of the Rule of Taizé, a Protestant monastic community in France. I followed this as I read some commentaries on the Rule of Saint Benedict, letting the words dwell in me.

I discovered that other lay people had also found that the Benedictine Way offered a balance for their complex and fragmented lives. Some had been on this particular path for a long time. Esther de Waal is an Anglican whose writings about the Benedictine Way are being read by both monastic and lay people.[20] Kathleen Norris, a Protestant, reflects on her experience as an oblate, a lay person who is associated with a Benedictine monastery, in her books *Dakota* and *The Cloister Walk*.

Through my reading of contemporary monastics and lay people, I learned more about the three vows at the heart of Benedictine spirituality. They offered me a grounding for a more balanced way to live my life. These are the vows of stability—meaning staying present to the life where you are—the vow of "continual conversion of life" that can be understood as "living open to change," and the vow of obedience or "listening to God."[21]

When I talked with my friend, who lives these vows and is committed to a contemplative way of life, I spoke of my fragmentation and my need to pace myself in ways that would help me live more fully where I am. Beneath my words she heard a longing for "a deepening of my union with God" and suggested that I might commit myself to some specific practice that would lead to this end. Her words helped name my longing and I liked her idea.

It made sense to me, so I named the elements that I would need to support me: meditation, intercessory prayer, spiritual reading, and eucharist or communion. Together we drew up a statement of my intention and designed a service of commitment to this practice for one year. That evening as I walked with my husband to meet our friend and celebrate my commitment in a simple service of thanksgiving, my eyes filled with tears. "This is very important to me. She has taken me seriously."

We continued our sabbatical journey and spent two weeks at a Quaker center for contemplation and study. There I rediscovered the writings of Gabriel Marcel, a Christian existentialist, who understood the human condition as "being on the way." He saw each of us as a traveler, yet deeply connected to our own particular place and life situation. Marcel commented that if he tried to separate himself from his life situation he would "destroy the deeply experienced bonds of intimacy which connect me to my world." The conditions of his life, family, vocation, and situation were "places not only of my participation in the mystery of being, but of my encounter with God."[22]

The first time that I read his words I felt a strong Yes! Marcel spoke of always being on a journey and yet at the same time being very present to where you are. This paradox underscored the importance of the phrase that had been inside of me. Going deep in the familiar was one way to be both present and at the same time open to the journey. His words offered an encouragement to dig more deeply into my own experience with the intensity of an archeologist.[23] I saw that my many roles actually provide opportunities to deepen my union with God.

I realized that the phrase to which I returned at the museum was kindred in spirit to Marcel and also to the vows at the core of Benedictine community life. As we prepared to return home to life in our own community, I felt sparks of excitement. I was eager to explore the connection between the monastic vows and my particular life in the village.

Reflection

1. What is it like to have someone listen to you, hear the longing beneath your words, and take you seriously? Have you experienced this?

2. A journal can be a place to hear ourselves and our longings, a place to take ourselves seriously. Have you used your journal this way recently?

10

BONDS OF INTIMACY

A familiar is a noun: a person, place, or thing; an animal or any part of creation that is part of our daily life. It can be a situation, an emotional state, or a relationship. A familiar can be as intimate as our own body.

Today I am aware of my aching head, a frequent companion during my passage through menopause. I decide to try to walk it off. I have been inwardly wrestling with a difficult situation, trying to solve too much with my head. I know this pattern well. When I recognize a familiar, I am at a choice point. I have options. I can view it as an ever present part of the unchanging landscape or I can try to see it in a new light. I can consciously push it away and ignore it or I can choose to get better acquainted with it and go deeper.

This practice of going deep with a familiar does not come naturally to me when I am confronted by difficulty. Part of me has an immediate reaction: "Get me out of here!" I sometimes make myself sick and that does it: I'm "out" for a while. This has been a pattern of escape for many years. When I cannot actually run away from a situation, I often spend mental and emotional energy fantasizing about fleeing. I have also experienced struggles that felt life threatening. When I have been in those deep emotional waters I have needed and found trusted companions, therapists, counselors, pastoral guides, and soul friends to accompany me while I am there.

My challenge involves learning how to stay with a difficult situation by going beneath the surface. In *The Journal of a Solitude*, May Sarton used the image of digging deep as she went below the surface of her familiar experience: being alone. "It always comes back to the same necessity: go deep enough and there is a bedrock of truth, however hard."[24]

The area for my excavation in these householding years is composed of my relationships, my body, and the elements of my day. They offer me opportunities to learn about how to "be with" my life. Perseverance, however, is not easy for most of us. We may find different modes of escape. For me it has been flight into sickness. For others alcohol and other substances, food, frantic exercise, and ceaseless activity can also be forms of flight.

In this culture of rapid change and impermanence, it is encouraging to know that in the fifth century, Benedict of Nursia, the founder of Benedictine communities, recognized a common inclination toward escape from difficulty. One of the three vows made by those who enter this community is the vow of stability, to "stand still" rather than run; to consciously choose to be right where you are. The monastic commitment to stability "relates primarily to persons and not simply to place . . . it is a matter of commitment to situations and persons."[25] Esther de Waal adds a further level to this understanding as she reflects on stability in her book *Living with Contradiction:*

> The vow of stability tells me that I must not run away from myself. It tells me to stand still, to stand firm . . . in the fundamental sense of standing still in my own center, not trying to run away or escape from myself, the person who I really am.[26]

This vow addresses my soul work. "The quality of soul is the quality of depth," Sister Donald Corcoran commented in a talk on Soul and Spirit. She was speaking with a group of Benedictine oblates, lay people engaged in living out the Benedictine Way in their own lives. "To grow as a soulful person means to grow in human heartedness, in depth and interiority and in a greater and greater capacity for the Spirit."[27]

Soul work develops that capacity for the Spirit. Going deep in the familiar is a form of soul work, which can open space within us for the Spirit to move more freely in and through our lives. Both Saint Benedict and Gabriel Marcel mention the condition of human openness as essential for growth. "Availability," Marcel's word, involves a willingness to go beneath the known. We begin with a conscious choice. It is a commitment to be present to this person, this situation, this pain, or this behavior, trusting that the Spirit can be in the midst of it, even though there may be no immediate evidence. Walking step-by-step through our circumstances is a way to live out the vow of stability.

One night, after a particularly hard day for both of us, my husband said, "This is one way to go deep in the familiar—being married thirty-five years." Long-term marriage or relationship is indeed a familiar that presents challenges for growth in soulfulness. The patterns of relating that develop over the years become so familiar that we often live them out again and again. "We've been here before . . ." is sometimes accompanied by a sigh. "Let's just get through this one more time . . ." is often a decision that is made by both partners without communicating that choice to each other.[28]

Our marriage and family life has been the place from which I have wanted to run the most. The more intimate the bonds, the more painful the struggles. Scenes from early years flash through

my mind; I feel again my extreme frustration with the circumstances of our life. There was the night that I threw the dishes
across the kitchen, grabbed my car keys, and bolted out the door
of our little ranch-style parsonage. I left behind three young children and a husband to pick up the pieces. As I drove up and
down back roads, my mind was frantically trying to pull together
fragments of thoughts and feelings. I wanted out! I did not want
to return to the well-known setting of my daily life.

Finally I came home. Walking in the door was a choice, as was
my explanation to the children that my explosion had to do with
me and not with them. Then came the excavation work with my
husband. What is really going on for me...for you...beneath
the surface? Can we really listen to each other or will we only
be hearing our own story? Do we need someone else to help us
hear each other? Can we risk the vulnerability of sharing in this
way and then allow for the empty space of not knowing and the
possibility of healing? Can we grow in soulfulness through this
painful time?

A mutual choice to dig beneath the surface of a familiar pattern
in a relationship usually comes when we are in a stuck place. It
might be a present painful experience, past shared memory, or
anxiety about the future. It requires at least these three qualities.

- Willingness to look at the source of our reactions: Where
  did that come from in me?

- Openness to really listen, a kind of listening with reverence
  for the other's experience as well as our own.

- Trusting that in the space of mutual vulnerability, the Spirit
  is at work to free us both to be more fully who we are in
  relation to one another.

Often a trusted guide is helpful for this kind of depth work: a therapist, clergy person, counselor, or soul friend. When we do soul work separately or together, we need to give ourselves time.

> The process is ongoing
> It cannot be rushed.
> Going deep involves staying power,
> awareness . . . presence
> being with
> returning again and again.

My father reflected on fifty years of marriage and wrote these words as part of a celebration statement. In many ways they speak of the staying power of the vow of stability.

> Fifty years of marriage is something quite different from the sheer length of the years. It is the essence of a journey that spans uphills and downhills, goals achieved; unexpected joys, and times of failure, disappointments, and offenses that sought forgiveness.
>
> The thirteenth chapter of Corinthians is not just for reading at weddings. It is a discipline and a constant for the days and years. Love is not arrogant or rude, love glories not in one-upmanship or being right, love suffers and is kind, love hangs in there. And ultimately this delicate, gentle, but tough bond supersedes all else and becomes the one imperishable gift we can have if we are humble enough to receive it.[29]

In a long-term marriage, every now and then partners feel bored with each other: "It is the same old thing." In a culture that puts a high priority on novelty, marriage does involve much that is repetitive. The many years of shared life, however, provide us the opportunity to grow in depth.

There was a time when our marriage felt boring. It was not something either one of us wanted to admit. Fortunately, my dreams often get my attention when I am trying to deny something. The images and sometimes the puns succeed in awaking me to what is so. The dream was simple:

> We are in a lush greenhouse. It is warm.
> There are several isles of tables with plants and flowers.
> There are boards placed between the tables, resting on the tables.
> C. and I are there, each lying on a board.

The message from my dreaming self seems pretty clear. We are in a setting that is a lush place of potential growth. We are resting in an in-between place, each on a board/bored. Our boredom is a place of choice; the potential is there. The dream sets the stage for the question: What do you want to do about it?

I had first to acknowledge to myself that I had felt bored before. My recognition made this moment in time a choice point for me. Do I want to go deeper with this which I have been denying? Do I want to blame it on my husband or on our marriage? Can I own that I am creating my boredom? Where does this come from in me? Am I willing to explore it? How do I do it?

First I have to choose to get better acquainted with the behavior that I am experiencing, so I begin by observing myself. When I feel bored or boring in social situations, I pull into myself and do not speak my thoughts and feelings. This for me is a form of running away. Instead of coming forth myself, I become the good listener, an easy role for me. However, I am not fully engaged because I am also listening to an inner commentary that competes with being fully present.

Within, I hear comments like these: That woman is so smart, how effective she must be in her work, she is really making a difference in people's lives. . . . How boring I am! I have nothing to add to this conversation . . . and besides, nobody is drawing me out.

At that point I recognize a childlike tone. I picture a little one grabbing my skirt and whining because she can't yet say: "Please pay attention to me. I want to be included." This childlike response raises a flag for me. I need to check in with myself. I can choose to actually leave this setting for a while in order to connect with my adult perspective on what is going on. This is a strategy for "standing still in my own center."

When I do remove myself from the situation for a moment of reflection, which is different than running away, I become aware of another familiar behavior. I am withholding myself because I want someone to recognize who I am beneath my surface. I want that kind of attention. After many years of looking for this from others, I now realize that I am the one who needs to pay attention to this longing. I need to listen within and be open to seeing what I can change in the situation. I need to find ways and settings where I can come forth more fully. I am the one to tend the flame.

As I reflect on this soul work, I see the healthy interconnection of the Benedictine vows. Standing still in one's center also involves a choice to be open to change by listening on the deepest level. Often I cannot do this kind of soul work until after the event. Then I use my journal to connect with the childlike part of me that reacts to such encounters. I write a dialogue with her as a way to find out how she is feeling. This writing adds to my understanding and often my intention to make different choices when similar circumstances arise. And they do. We get presented with what we need to help us grow in soulfulness, which truly is growth in "human heartedness" and does create "capacity for Spirit."

Boredom led me to a recognition of my need to express and use my gifts in ways that are appropriate for me. Holding back only shut me down and affected my most intimate relationship and all my other relationships as well. When I was blaming my husband and our marriage for my boredom, my dreaming self challenged me to look at what I was doing. It offered me the promise that when I took responsibility for my own choices there would be lush potential for growth.

Another time my husband and I feared that the crucible of our marriage could not contain the intensity of our struggle; several years afterward we spoke together of the days and months that it took to work our way through that particular challenge.

> With gentle hands
> we touch back to that painful time
> sensing that the wound has healed.
> Such touching only brushes
> the scar
> rekindling memories
> that enflame but briefly.

> We have traveled far for this return
> and now can dwell here
> long enough
> to add our oil of healing
> then move on
> to gratitude
> for that which we have gone through
> and have gained.

Reflection

1. What is your mode of escape when you feel like running away from a situation that is difficult for you? Does that mode serve you?

2. Recall a situation in which you were or are enabled to "stand still" and firm in your own center while walking through hard times step-by-step. How did you do this?

RITUALS OF RETURNING

Most of us choose to return to that which we love, to people, places, conditions which we already know to be life-giving and restoring. Our longing for sacred space leads us to return to these renewing experiences, for they connect us with our soul. Many of us are "wearied by the changes and chances of this life," and without our conscious awareness we are creating our own rituals of returning to touch the "eternal changelessness."[30]

"Ritual creates a context for reconnecting with the seat of our souls."[31] Our son discovered this as he described his yearly return to a mountain in New Hampshire. "For years I've been making an unconscious pilgrimage to Mount Adams. It began simply as a physical challenge—How long would it take me to run to the summit and back?" Now in his mid-thirties, he reflects on his experience.

Every year since 1984, I've made a pilgrimage to Mount Adams. At first I didn't know it was a pilgrimage. It was simply a physical challenge to see how long it would take me to run to the summit and back. Later, it became something more—a force that drew me each summer like a magnet.

Mount Adams is my favorite summit in New Hampshire's White Mountains. It is less-traveled than its neighboring peaks and seems remote and a bit mysterious to me. The trail I take begins on the north side of the mountain. It is rugged and steep in places, but rewards you with spectacular views from a knife ridge above the tree line.

I grew up spending summers in the White Mountains, and this annual run is a return to happy memories. It is a chance to smell fir trees again, feel squishy moss underfoot, and touch the ancient New Hampshire granite that to me has always represented permanence and stability. Even more, my run is an escape from the world—a small adventure to a blustery summit from which, when it is clear, you can see Canada.

Though I've hiked Mount Adams with others, I always do the run alone. It is familiar ground, and I know to back off when the weather gets bad. It is a way for me to vanish from the face of the earth, if only for a few hours. Sometimes, as I run, I chuckle and feel like a child playing hide-and-seek with the rest of the world.

In an unexpected way, my Mount Adams run has become a ritual. I suppose that someday I won't be able to run up the mountain. But I will continue to hike it just the same.

As I get older, buffeted by life's surprises, Mount Adams is an anchor.

In this ritual Jim connects with "permanence and stability," the rock-like qualities of soul home.

A friend with whom I visit each summer told me about a daily ritual which she and her ninety-year-old Aunt Maggie shared. For several years, while my sixty-year-old friend was companion to her aunt, they would walk. Each day, weather permitting, they would make their way out into their field to sit on a bench.

We were silent and warm. Together gazing at the so familiar scene—favorite birches, grasses gently bending in the breeze, late afternoon backlighting the dark pine grove, clusters of flies hanging in the air, cats stalking insects. We are not walking to the bench now, except in my memory, and will not walk there together next spring either. My aunt is in bed following a stroke, peacefully dying at home. So this is a returning in memory.

I shared this memory with Maggie. She likes the idea of the ritual of returning. Together we read the words from Isaiah 30:16a: In returning and rest you shall be saved; in quiet and in trust shall be your strength.

"I like that," she said. "Returning and rest is what it was walking to the bench."

"What makes a ritual of returning different from being stuck in a rut?" I asked my friend. "Love," she answered.

You go to be with something you love and you go out to love it. Many times it would be tedious, Maggie's ways and pace are slower, our interests are different. I had to move through that. I ended up being patient. Going through the tedium and out the other side drew out the love.

To go to be with something you love is the way that we go to our family retreat each year in August. Both as a child and as an adult, I have always lived in a parsonage which belonged to the church. When my parents found a small farmhouse in northern New Hampshire and brought it back to life with love and hard work, it became the first constant place in the life of our family. When my husband and I arrive now for our time alone, it usually takes a few days to let the mountain rhythm take over. Exhaustion.

Falling asleep over lunch, over dinner. Then slowly I begin to focus on just one thing at a time.

> A journey
> to the mailbox
> and back.

The healing rhythm deepens as my awareness heightens. I become more fully present as I mindfully return to these simple tasks.

> Washing by hand
> these four things
> a full day's work.

In the act of hanging out the few clothes needed here, I feel the hot sun and swirling mountain air. With time to reflect, I recall the years when our children were with us: First we hung out diapers; later, sleeping bags. Now children are having children and hanging out their clothes. All is connected through this line...years of constant community and now solitude. I see a hawk above me and remember other days of high winds when the cry of a hawk has pierced my solitary time.

> On my way
> to the clothesline
> I hear a cry.

> Eyes upturned
> I catch the beginning
> of a hawk's spiral flight.

> Following it
> against sun and cloud
> I trace the slow ascent,

> For a moment
> I turn to hang my shirt
> losing her . . . until
>
> I see
> a distant speck
> folding into clouds.

I cherish these times of solitude and personal rituals which con-nect me with my soul home. No wonder I am drawn to a Benedictine order, which honors the need to balance commu-nity with solitude. Life here in this place moves back and forth between both. Right now it provides the opportunity to learn how to be in community with four generations together at one time. We range in age from three months to ninety. In many places in the world, this way of living is an everyday reality: all generations under one roof. For us it is a unique time each year.

We have developed rituals as we have shared this sacred space over thirty-five years. Our children, now adults, still return to them for a sense of continuity and connection. Since the earliest years, a simple practice has marked our arrival each summer. As we approach well-known landmarks, the car finally turns onto our dirt lane, the excitement mounting as we pass our neighbors' houses. The driver honks through the field that fronts the house until the car stops. After welcoming hugs from my parents, we each make our way, running, walking, or carrying a child, to the standpipe in the field. An ever-flowing source of springwater pours continuously from its spout. A tin dipper hangs from the pipe. The cold, fresh water splashes us as we take our first drinks of the season.

A ritual has also evolved for leaving at the end of a vacation. Whether it has been for a week or an overnight, those who stay behind wave goodbye until the car is out of sight. The travelers wave their hands out the windows until the car moves through the trees. The driver honks the horn as the car rounds the bend in the lane. We are saying goodbye with awareness; we allow the taste of letting go to linger.

Letting go means change. Accepting change makes space for something new. For many years my mother rose early to walk before fixing breakfast with my father. In her mid-eighties, she had to change her routine. These words have helped her to accept such changes. "The edge of eighty is not reached without some reminders that the body is not a permanent habitation."[32] She developed a new practice, one that fit the present, agreeing with Esther de Waal who spoke of aging as "a narrowing down of possibilities and yet at the same time an invitation to go deeper into reality."[33]

> When it became more difficult to take my regular morning walk around the pond and back, I began going up the road to the bridge over our lovely brook. Here, leaning against the sturdy wooden rail, I saw and heard and felt the magic, the mystery of ongoing, ever-flowing, sparkling clear water from somewhere up there—out of a mountainside, never ceasing, ancient yet crystal new and full of lights.
>
> In changing days it will be my privilege to see Fall's colors begin in the green banks' growth, and to listen for new notes in the sounds of the brook, and in the patterns of its journey. I will keep returning to that place to stop, look, and listen; to be at peace, to say "Thank You."

For me it is hard to accept the "changing days" as a child with aging parents and as a parent with children who are now parents.

Part of me resists and holds onto the way it has been. My grasp often gets tighter as I see things changing. I resist what is so and place myself in conflict so that I am anxious and not fully present. I know I must pay attention to my anxiety when I wake abruptly in the night with shortness of breath and with my mind grasping for ways to control events that "might" happen.

I need to get beneath my agitation to my sadness about letting go of what has been. So many changes in everyone's lives put me in touch with our mortality and with death itself. Letting go of what was is a form of dying. The Benedictine Way recognizes the necessity of this kind of dying, dying in order that change and inner transformation can take place.

This is the heart of the vow of *conversatio morum*, "an archaic phrase" which defies translation, according to Esther de Waal, but "brings the demand for continuous change . . . a modern re-writing of the vows simply calls it the vow of openness."[34] This second monastic vow of openness to change seems to provide a vital balance for the vow of stability. For Thomas Merton it was "the most mysterious of our vows" and "actually the most essential" because "it can be interpreted as a commitment to a total inner transformation of one sort or another."[35] It therefore involves various forms of dying.

This summer I have been reading T. T. Williams's *Refuge: An Unnatural History of Family and Place*. As a daughter and a naturalist, Williams records her journey as she faces loss and death itself, again and again. She is no longer able to turn for refuge to the familiar: to her mother or to her grandmother, both of whom have breast cancer, or to the creatures of her homeland, whose habitat is being destroyed. She discovers her refuge to exist in her "capacity to love. If I can learn to love death, then I can begin to feel refuge in change."[36] Perhaps, if I learn to love death—in all

its forms, minor and major—then I can live my way into the vow
of openness to change. Love is the way.

IT IS NIGHT IN THE MIDDLE OF AUGUST, after a day in which I
felt caught between the generations. My heart feels stretched by
the needs of many. I wake abruptly. My mind begins to spin with
anxious questions. Will this be the kind of time needed by my
children who arrived so stressed and exhausted? Will my parents
be well enough to stay on into the fall without us? Will the lump
in my daughter's breast continue to shrink? What if it doesn't?
How are these young people going to make it in this economy?
Will they have to work into their seventies? Will they have security in their old age; for that matter, will we? Will we be able
to carry on the stewardship of this home and land financially
when it is passed on to us? What will we have to pass on to
our children?

I feel an escalation of sensations in my body as my anxiety
heightens. I want to cry, give release to my frustrations and my
fears. The walls are too thin to let the sobs come, so I go to
the window and send them out into the darkness. I have no
place to run. I pick up my icon of Mary—it is called "Mother
of Loving-kindness." She is holding the infant Jesus tenderly to
herself as he is touching her face in a most intimate moment.
I have kept this small icon by my bed ever since my therapist
suggested that I keep it close for moments like this. Out of his
own experience, he knew the importance of a visible, tangible
sign of the loving embrace, which my fearful child and panicky
adult needed.[37]

Now as I lie back down to sleep, I hold it to my heart. I pray for
Mary's embracing love to enfold me and all those whom I love. I
return to the words that I memorized long ago from the Revised

Standard Version of the Bible: "Underneath are the everlasting arms" (Deut. 33:27b). The phrase becomes my mantra as I breathe my way back to sleep. I have learned in the past, when my energy has been depleted and anxious thoughts start to escalate, that this practice helps me re-turn to the sacred, to the source of my being. This tangible holding of the icon to my heart is a way to return to love.

Embraced in the night by a love bigger than my own, I return the next morning to the familiar, to be present to what is: my changing, growing family as we are right now. I am grateful for the night's healing, the inner release of my panicky grasp. I finally feel open to changing my perceptions and freed to go out and love what is, as my friend expressed it. I recall the words that I found once while on retreat with the Sisters of Providence: "Embrace the present moment as an ever-flowing source of holiness."

This morning I do that. My two-year-old grandson and I walk to the standpipe in the field. Springwater gushes forth from its spout and we reach for the metal dipper with its long handle. "Water," he says. We fill the cup. He drinks and holds it out again. "More water." I ask him to let me drink. He tips the cup to my lips. A Chinese proverb says, "Whenever you drink, remember the source," and I do with deep gratitude. We say, "Thank you, water," deep down Living Water.

Reflection

1. In what circumstances is it hardest for you to accept change?

2. Consider the Celtic root of the verb "to change." It comes from the word that means exchange: to give up something for something else. Write or reflect on change in your life from this perspective.

3. Reflect on simple rituals in your life that help you to return to your center in the midst of change.

12

LISTENING THROUGH THE FAMILIAR

Our vacation ends tomorrow. It is always an act of discipline to get into the car and leave the mountains. In four hours time we reach the highway that circles Boston. Each year as we merge into the fast-moving traffic, my inner pace picks up.

In conversation with a friend not long ago, I voiced my love of the summer pace of life and my resistance to the approach of the fall. She offered an insight that came out of her reflection on this time of year.

As I sat on my porch watching a dry leaf fall from the maple tree and observing the sharp contrast of lengthening shadows and sunlight, I felt a mood shift from the lively activity of summer to a more reflective, gentle time, a gradual slipping inward for the winter months to come.

How odd, I thought, that in all the years of being a student and then a teacher, that we had to gear up to expectations, new beginnings, feeling performance anxiety, just as our bodies and souls and our natural environment were winding down, settling in, mellowing out. No wonder we groan at that transition!

I am aware of how my own anxiety escalates when I place myself in conflict with the pace that is appropriate for me. Many other New Englanders express anxiety around Labor Day. It may in part be a consequence of our lack of harmony with autumn's natural movement of preparation for the quiet of winter.

I am savoring this last day of our vacation as I read by the window of our cabin that looks out on the brook. On the sill of the wide window my father painted the words: STOP, LOOK, AND LISTEN, words of his father who used them to get the attention of my brother and me as children when we were going too fast.

The call to listen comes to me also from another source, kindred in spirit to that of my grandfather. I am reading commentaries on the Rule of Saint Benedict, which begins with the word "Listen." "Listen carefully, my children, to my instructions, and attend to them with the ear of your heart."[38] This call to stop and pay attention introduces the third vow of obedience as "the willingness to listen for the voice of God in life."[39]

Obedience has not been a favorite word of mine. According to Esther de Waal, our word comes from the Latin *oboedire*, which shares its root with *audire*, to hear. "It is the listening of the whole person, of body as well as intellect, and it requires love as well as cerebral assent, and it also involves mindfulness, an awareness which turns listening from a cerebral activity into a living response."[40]

My response of the moment is: enough words! I walk out into the field to be in the sun. I listen. There are crickets all around me. How did that happen? Yesterday at this time of day, as I remember, it was quiet, a lazy August afternoon. Today, late afternoon is filled with cricket sounds. When did they begin? Have they been building up to this crescendo for a while and have I chosen not to hear?

Like the sounds of crickets, I have not always been aware of the signs of my escalating anxiety. In the middle of my householding years, my father spoke to me of his father, whose words "stop, look, and listen" have become for me a call to a more contemplative way of being. In his thirties and forties my grandfather had what was then called "nervous breakdowns," extended periods of anxiety and depression. When I was that same age my father wanted me to know that it might be "in the genes," as he, too, deals with anxiety. This opened up new awareness and a sense of connection between the generations. It was also an encouragement to pay attention to anxiety when I experienced it.

I now recognize the particular signs of my anxiety: certain kinds of dreams, abrupt waking in the middle of the night, shortness of breath, a grabbing in my chest, and sometimes the speeding up of my heart. These act as red flags for me. They get my attention and at that point I need to *stop:* to acknowledge the symptoms and take the time needed to attend to them. This is another form of tending the flame.

I have learned, for instance, that my body is getting my attention through my shortness of breath. I know that anxiety can escalate with lack of oxygen so I begin to take long, rhythmic breaths. If I can, I walk or swim. Exercise draws on deep breathing and helps to move energy that is "stuck." I know that my symptoms usually begin when I feel a loss of control. So I use my journal to move out the thoughts that are going around in my head. It is one way to pay attention to what is happening on a deeper level. The week before Christmas, when I was very anxious, I used my journal in this way:

> My familiar: anxiety! Got to get things done:
> Letter about work, gifts; buying presents!
> At the same time my familiar: wanting!
> Wanting to be present, be a presence,
> in the Presence . . .

Right now:
        breathing in . . . breathing out . . . into my belly.

It has taken time and willingness to become acquainted with this anxious conflicted condition that is my occasional companion. In the process I have learned that anxiety can provide an opening for soul work and an opportunity to practice deep listening. For Thomas Moore, author of *Care of the Soul,* anxiety and other emotional conditions can "come as alternatives to the plans we have" and offer "wonderful material for the soul."[41]

Many years ago I entered college with some real fears about myself as a student. I soon convinced myself that I was there by mistake and that my scholarship had been given to me because of my family's record of service and not for my merit. I was sure that it would be discovered that I could not keep up and that I would flunk out by January. I found it increasingly hard to be in social situations. "Please pass the butter" took concentrated effort.

My fears fed the nighttime anxieties that escalated until the dean of students, alerted by my parents who sensed my inner desperation, called me into her office and drew me out. In that caring connection, I felt the first ease of my panic. With that conversation, a slow process of learning about anxiety began. I realized how important it is when I am inside anxiety to connect with others "outside" to see myself in a larger context.

When I am working through anxiety now, my objective is also to get to the observer place within me. From there I can *look* from the center of myself and recognize that there are parts of me that get anxious in certain circumstances. I hear them inside voicing their fears. The anxious thoughts escalate, full of words that build on each other as they did that summer night not long ago when our four-generation family was together. This "inner talk," referred to by Robert Gerzon in his book *Finding Serenity in the Age of Anxiety*, can be creatively engaged through dialogue.[42]

If I do not stop and take a look at what is going on inside, the inner talk increases, absorbs, and sometimes immobilizes me. Therefore, I have learned to have dialogues with various parts of myself. A familiar part is the one that I call Boney Joanie. This inner critic feels very thin, angular, and harsh. Her critical message for whatever situation is scaring me at the time is: *You are not enough!* Within my mind I hear all the reasons why I am inadequate. Through journal dialogue, my training as a therapist, and my own therapy, I have discovered that behind this negative critic is a frightened child who needs encouragement and reassurance when venturing into new situations. In the process of working with her, I have found dialogue to be a valuable tool for engaging my fears directly.

However, when I am in the middle of the squall of my anxiety, it is hard work to get to the observer place. I get there and then I get pulled back. It is helpful in these times to find someone to be a companion while I do this kind of inner work: a therapist, counselor, clergyperson, or soul friend: a companion who is on land watching, looking out for me, encouraging me while I navigate my boat in the offshore emotional and spiritual squall.

I have also learned that another level of anxiety confronts us with our own mortality. This often lies underneath the apparent disturbance. I need to be willing to look below the initial stimulus and to *listen* beneath the surface anxiety to a deeper voice which raises issues of meaning and purpose for my life.[43] When I take the time to do so, I discover that I have been making choices that are in conflict with my true nature.

Several years ago, I went through a period of anxiety that lasted about three months. As painful and frightening as that time was, it was an experience that, in retrospect, gave me an opportunity to learn about stability, openness to change, and listening. By not running from my fear of change, I was able to listen to God in the midst of that hard time. I discovered the sacred at the deepest level of my anxiety, which led me to further explorations in my own inner work and with others. For this learning, I am grateful. However . . . it is a hard way to travel.

That spring, events and situations in my personal life converged to create several challenges that once again raised my fear of not being enough. In my work life as a therapist and as a consultant, there were situations in which I felt caught between the expectations and commitments of others and my own sense of the truth. I felt increasing tension within me as I tried to clarify my role in each situation. It took a great deal of time and energy. Often in the middle of the night I would wake with my fears. I wrote:

> Feeling caught between two adversaries. No win! My skills and abilities are not enough to turn this situation around. It feels like a setup for frustration and a sense of failure.

I was also anticipating our youngest daughter's wedding. I had difficulty accepting my new role as "mother of the bride." That title became a symbol for the ending of my years of motherhood; it was accompanied by the hormonal changes of my peri-menopausal body, all of which touched off some real grief. But there was no time for reflection.

I had bouts of laryngitis throughout the spring. I had to force myself to eat. Often I would wake with hot flashes and then not be able to sleep. As I lay in bed my thoughts would escalate in intensity, so I would get up and, once again by candlelight, write in my journal, moving the surface fears out and onto the page. As

I read my journals now, I notice the process of going deeper as I named my fears.

> I am scared. I've been up for hours—awake—imagining go-ing into the hospital with a breakdown. What's breaking down is me trying to do it all well, perfectly—the way I *want* to be and the reality seems so far from there. HELP me to let go of these killing expectations!

This cry for help evoked another voice inside me.

> The Lord is my shepherd. The Shepherd will supply my needs. I cannot live on my own. My life IS unmanageable. I have been away from my soul. Separated, trying to go it on my own without moment by moment acknowledging the Source of my being, without which I can do nothing.

This moved into a prayer and a naming of my deepest fear.

> Apart from you I am a wasteland
> and I fear for my life.

It was at this point that I realized that beneath my panic about my job situation and deeper than my fear of not being enough for the tasks that were in front of me, my soul cried for help.

> My soul is waking me up in the middle of the night.
> It needs attention. It needs time. I need to listen.

I was able to give it time. I lost my voice completely from not sleeping. I have since learned that one of the main causes of anxiety is fatigue. What a vicious cycle that can be. I also had been steadily losing weight and felt weak. Once again my body was the means through which I learned what was needed. I stayed home to listen with the ear of my heart.

One night a wave of volcanic fear hit me. A friend of mine had recently died of cancer. My fears that night became catastrophic; anxiety became panic. I truly feared for my own life. My panicky inner child had taken over with her fear of failing or going under, which to me always feels like drowning.

In the morning I called my therapist and got to his office, not knowing if I could make it home. At this point I was hardly eating and feared dying because of lack of nourishment. He encouraged me to go deeper and to recognize another part of myself. "The undernourished part of you is coming to the surface in this time of letting go. You are not cracking up or going crazy but opening up to something new: a new way of nourishing yourself."

It was at this time that he suggested that I use the icon of Mary to keep with me, to touch and hold as I needed it—a very tangible reminder of the presence of the Mother of Loving-kindness. The young/old mother's eyes look out into the suffering that she knows already and will know in the future as she holds the young child in a most tender embrace. Listening to my anxiety "with the ear of my heart," as Saint Benedict said, did lead to a deeper level. It opened me to my soul's longing to touch and be touched in the embrace of the Holy One.

Listening also led me to action. I have since recognized that action is a way to ground what we have learned by listening with our soul entire. The action that we choose may appear on the surface to be a simple thing. Others may not be aware of its significance, but it is essential that we recognize its importance. For me to buy a dress as the "mother of the bride" was a major step—literal and symbolic. I marked this in writing:

I searched for and found a dress. It is my personal statement of acceptance. I want to embrace my part in this

life-changing event, to move with the life energy of this
event and with the movement of the Spirit on my life
journey.

I also came to a decision about one of my jobs. I recorded this in
my journal.

> I will not take on the role that I am being asked to take.
> More is needed than I am trained to do. It is beyond the
> scope of my job as defined. I am willing to lose the job that
> I love if that is the cost of speaking the truth. If they must
> hire someone else, then so be it.

I wrote a letter stating what I could do. I owned my limitations
and my willingness to give the job to someone with specific qual-
ifications. There was great release in coming to this decision. The
energy that had been caught up in indecision was freed to work
cooperatively with others who were involved in the situation. Although I worked myself out of a job, the joint solution had integrity
and opened the way for a new form of work for me. The gift from
this time in my life was a learning.

When I awake suddenly with anxious thoughts and the fear of
being caught in the web of anxiety again, there are ways that I
can walk through this familiar experience. I now know that the
path through this dark valley actually can lead me closer to the
Holy One and to my true self.

I am grateful for much in this "education of the heart." I thank
my father for his openness and honesty about his battles with
anxiety. I thank my grandfather for his words that guide me now
as I work with my own anxiety. I use them to remind me of what
I have learned.

STOP with the red flag of your particular signs of anxiety.

> Do not push on with your life. Pay attention.
>
> Is this anxiety which you can and need to act on?
>
> Or is it a flag alerting you to the fact that you are in conflict with your true being?
>
> If it is the latter, you can choose to work with yourself.

LOOK at what is right in front of you.

> Sort it out in your journal.
>
> Make a determination.
>
> If it moves you to action, do it.
>
> If your energy feels stuck or intensifies, know that somewhere you are in conflict.
>
> Observe and work with the parts of yourself that are fearful.
>
> It is worth taking the time to do this soul work.

LISTEN by being open to what your deeper self is saying to you. Hear with your whole self.

> Let your body, mind, and spirit be receptors for this soul level of listening.
>
> Be willing to "listen for the voice of God in life."
>
> Know that it will mean acting on what you learn.
>
> It may mean making some changes.

Reflection

1. What in your life right now is an old familiar that offers you the opportunity to "listen to God"? It might be a circumstance involving a relationship, a work situation, a health problem, an emotion, etc.

2. What are the ways that you have found to listen, ways that have deepened your union with God by attending "with the ear of your heart" in the midst of this circumstance?

13

MONET IN THE 1990s

My experience at the museum has been with me through this decade. Images of the haystacks are on my walls and in my mind's eye. I am still discovering the meaning of the call to go deep in the familiar, Monet's gift to me.

As I walk each morning I return to places that I love. On this "well-worn walk," as Thoreau would call it, I note the season's subtle changes. I marvel at the gift of sight, sound, smell, touch, and taste as I stand on the Headlands looking out to sea. The rugged point of granite rock, berry bushes, and gnarled trees stands at the entry to Sandy Bay Harbor. I scan the shoreline for symbols of my present life: the town built around the harbor, the road to the parsonage where our three children grew and others come and go, the roof of the school where I taught, and the steeple of the church above the rooftops. They are all reminders of the community that provides the counterpart to my solitude.

I turn to look at an area on this rock cap, which in early spring supports a vernal pond. The vegetation is still blackened from last summer's forest fire. Even so, green shoots of wild iris are pushing up through the charred remains. Birds are everywhere, like old friends also returning to this homing place. One bird in particular seems to demand my attention each morning. He becomes my

teacher. He is a mockingbird who seems to sing as if driven by the
next call, next call, next call.

> To the listener your song brings cheer
>> but to the singer
>> there may be no rest
>> while you perform
>> the voices of others.
>
> Yet the song is yours
>> and well it may be
>> that you enjoy
>> each new call.
>
> But I
>> I need to stay with one
>> and deeply go
>> with that single call.

I listen with the ear of my heart and dip into my memory
of Monet's ritual of returning, which enabled him to know his
subjects as familiars. I remember the day at the art museum when
I stood with hundreds of others gazing at the haystack series. I was
in forest time then. Through Monet's paintings, for that moment
I was touched by the Eternal. This is the nature of forest time,
whether it is for moments, hours, or days.

Today on the Headlands the mockingbird reminds me to stay
with my practice, and that call continues to sing inside of me.

Reflection

What practice do you feel called to "stay with" that supports you
at this time in your life as a householder?

Part
III

TIME IN THE FOREST

A journey becomes a pilgrimage
when we are consciously engaged
in going to a center,
deliberately going into the center
with the purpose of going to the sacred center.

—Sister Donald Corcoran in conversation

14

A TIME APART

In the process of writing this section, I became aware that there are many aspects of time in the forest. There are a variety of experiences that lead us or sometimes catapult us into forest time. A holy moment alone on the beach may gently bring us to a deeper awareness of the Eternal in our life. A sudden job loss or illness may drive us into the wilderness of the unknown. There we are forced into growth by subtraction and forced to deepen our trust.

Time in the forest can take place in many settings. Common to all forest time experience is time alone. Solitude is at the core of this life rhythm. Sometimes being alone is a great and unexpected gift, like a snow day when we were school children. Most often, time for solitude has to be planned to fit around or in between the rest of our life.

> Morning is the best time
> preferably with the early sun rather than
> this season's early darkness.
> Early before the world awakens is my time for me.
> Solitude is the ingredient
> added to prayer
> and quiet
> that gives me nourishment and comfort.

Safe space
with candle lit,
a passage to read and take to my heart.
Eyes half closed
rest on my coffee cup's circle of white,
a symbol of life and warmth in my hand.[44]

Sometimes being alone echoes with emptiness and the "deep down dark of one by one," as Kathleen Norris names it.[45] This kind of solitude forces us to draw on spiritual practices that enable us to be present in those empty spaces. Beverly Williams's poetic reflection speaks of this.

Wilderness time may be space and time stretched
far ahead
into black darkness.
I gaze ahead
without knowledge
of what is held in that deep dark.
Breath/prayers turn black into a soft velvet cloak
spread out before me like an offering.[46]

"Wilderness," "the dark wood," or "arid desert" are words that describe one aspect of this essential rhythm that contributes to the balance of wholeness for us as women. To move into the unknown, to be open to the unfamiliar, we often find ourselves forced to go below the surface of spiritual practices that have sustained us. Going deep in these familiars is a way to be with the sacred while we journey through the wilderness.

We need time apart from our householding life of connection and responsibility to experience this balancing rhythm. Time in the forest was first described to me by Edith Sullwold, master therapist and teacher. It is time apart from our usual householder's life during which we engage in the process of "assimilation, distillation, and integration," she said. Time in the forest enables a person to return to the marketplace or village in order "to be there in a new way."

When one woman who is an artist heard this description she said, "Those big words: 'assimilate, distill, and integrate' don't speak to me." A poet in the group discussing forest time said:

> Think of it this way. It is like making soup. You gather in the food from the fridge or the garden. That is assimilation, a gathering in. Next, you throw the ingredients into a pot and cook them into a big soup. Slowly, lovingly, you distill it down to the essence, the base of the soup that is a blend of all the ingredients. Integration is the final product that has a life of its own, called soup. You drink it, take it into your being. The soup nourishes and adds to who you are. Then you share it with others, your friends and family. You bring it to your community.

This creative process can happen over time, like making soup, or in a brief moment when everything comes together, a moment of enlightenment. Forest time is not measured by length but by depth.

When we hold the sacred intent of the pilgrim who trusts that she is moving toward her own center and will find there the "Center of all centers,"[47] we can make choices for time apart. We can also choose to be awake and aware of the holy events and holy moments that take us deeper.

IN THE DARKNESS

It is a relief to be in darkness.

I boarded the bus at dusk. As we travel through the Pennsylvania hills, night comes. I have been at Kirkridge, a retreat center just off the Appalachian Trail near Stroudsburg, Pennsylvania. I led a weekend experience called "Time in the Forest: A Retreat for Midlife Women." Our ages ranged from forty to sixty-one. In both community and solitude for three days, we explored forest time. I am feeling gratitude for the people and the place. I also feel my tiredness as the bus carries me toward my own forest time at Transfiguration Monastery.

Little lights shine here and there in fields, dotting the hillsides. Night is settling in. It is quieting. I have the beginnings of a headache with familiar sensations, often my body's sign of letdown after a time of stimulation and connection. The hum of the motor and the soft overhead lights do not keep me from sinking into the darkness. I let my tired mind wander. With no agenda for this ride through the night, I open myself to memories and savor them.

I recall a bus trip several years ago. It was at the end of ten days which included leading another workshop at Kirkridge, family visits, a rendezvous with my husband in Philadelphia, a three-day retreat at Pendle Hill—a Quaker Center for study and contemplation—then I planned to go back to Kirkridge to attend a workshop on healing and finally, home. During the three days of retreat at Pendle Hill that I squeezed into my schedule, I never got to contemplation. I enjoyed being a student again with opportunity to listen, talk, and share ideas. However, I did not tend my need for solitude. The headache that plagued me during that time was my body saying *let down* and *stop.*

The day before I was to leave Pendle Hill for the final workshop at Kirkridge, I received a phone call saying that it was canceled due to the leader's illness. My flight home was not for five days. I felt my disappointment, but also my body's urgent need for quiet. "Could I just come and make a personal retreat for three days?" The answer was "You'll be on your own."

I would be alone. It was what I needed.

I arrived by bus and was taken to the cottage that stands at the edge of the forest. For the first time in days I allowed myself to settle into solitude. The birds slowly became quiet and dusk entered the little house. I could not bring myself to put lights on. Soon the lights of night herself spangled the sky. At one with the birds, I turned to my rest in the welcoming darkness.

Now as I travel through the darkness, en route once again to a time of personal retreat, I reflect on how it is that natural darkness has always felt like sacred space to me. I enter Forest Time as I pay attention to the memories that come.

As a seven-year-old I had the measles. As I lay for days in my bedroom with shades darkening the room, I knew that things were pretty serious, and yet I felt quieted and cooled. I think now of George Fox's words, "Be still and cool in thine own mind and spirit." The darkness was cooling, peace-giving. I felt safe.

Darkness also provided hiding places for me as a child: underneath the steps or in a huge wooden packing box, which served as a cabin that I shared with my brother. It was located at "Settler's Creek," otherwise known as our side yard. I recognize how blessed I was then to have a feeling of safety in the dark. Because I knew that there was light and security nearby, the pleasure of darkness was heightened.

As a young teenager, on vacation in Michigan, I was part of a group of kids who would often sleep out on the sand dunes near Lake Michigan. We told ghost stories until it got really dark. As we watched for shooting stars, we lay in bedrolls, more sandy than a sleeping bag ever could be. Finally, we tired ourselves out and people fell off to sleep. That was the time I loved best, when the talking had stopped and I could look up into the rich blue-black of night. It was that darkness that gave me permission as a teenager to simply be. Lying beneath the arching quiet, I felt that infinite depth soak down into me as I let go into sleep.

At nineteen, I had to take a summer off from my job to recuperate from pneumonia. For many days and nights, I rested and read poetry. I discovered Gerard Manley Hopkins, whose word rhythms and vivid images inspired me to try my own. I found an apple tree to which I returned each day to read and write. With the coming of night, I lay beneath the tree. I heard night sounds around me as I became still. The cadences of Hopkins echoed inside me. With dark ground beneath and the soft summer darkness wrapping round me, I absorbed the gift of darkness: permission to receive.

As a young mother, there were nights of rising to nurse a baby. Often resisting the call at first, I found that as my arms encircled my child for that most intimate moment, nothing else then seemed to matter. I was present to this new person with all my focus and attention. I felt the quiet of the night enfolding us both. Certainly there were times of numbness from exhaustion when I dozed as I provided the needed sustenance. And yet the darkness was always comforting and somehow replenishing for me as well. It gave me the opportunity to fill up my pores with silence. There was also space in the darkness for reflection, which was almost totally absent in the hours of light.

In the stillness I felt my connection with all who have held a child, longed for a child, or grieved for a child. The sacredness of that bond often led my thoughts to Mary. Her arms had also held a child whose life and death would embrace the light and the darkness of our world, and somehow she knew this in the depths of her heart where she, too, had pondered.

Darkness provides solitude for me, which is like the still pool at the center of the mythical forest in many fairy tales. I am drawn to find ways that get me there. There is an ancient monastic tradition that speaks of "blessed solitude." Monastery life recalls me to this pool at the center of my life. For this reason I journey once a year to Transfiguration Monastery. As I travel now through the darkness, I rest in solitude.

Reflection

For some people darkness is not welcoming. As Beverly Williams
wrote in her poem "Solitude":

> Darkness is not my friend
> does not offer solitude nor comfort
> but holds in it, sadness and loneliness
> confusion and alarm.
>
> Solitude may come in a bright form
> with breezes and sunshine, trees and rocks.
> These are my safe "solid"tude conditions.[48]

1. What provides solitude that feels like a blessing for you?
2. Is there a difference for you between solitude and loneliness?

16

GROWTH BY SUBTRACTION

The classical Hindu spiritual tradition recognizes the importance of time for reflection and replenishment of soul. Time in the forest is set apart from householding responsibilities and commitments to the community. During the period of forest time a person deepens his or her sense of union with the Divine through spiritual practices. Time in the forest is considered essential for discernment regarding the final stage of life.

Today in India some men and women enter this stage through a ceremony which recognizes that they have ended their householding years and are free to do what they choose to do in the next life phase. A husband and wife may choose to do different things. I met a man at Pendle Hill whose wife wanted to spend more time with her grandchildren. She went to live with her daughter for a time. He chose to come to the United States to study and experience community at the Quaker Center for Study and Contemplation. He planned to return to India and join his wife in establishing a self-sustaining community in their own country.

This contemporary expression of time in the forest is similar to that defined by Edith Sullwold, who described it as "time for assimilation, distillation, and integration." We need solitude to do this. We need time for the process of assimilating our life experience through remembering and reflection and then distilling what is truly important to us. The integration of our experience in the forest enables us to return to our life of connection with others in work, family, and community, and to "be there in a new way."[49]

In the traditional Hindu model when a man saw his son's sons, he would leave the village and literally go into the forest to stay there until he achieved mystical union. Then he would journey through the land as a holy man. This ancient tradition presents a linear and predictable progression from the student to the house-holder, who then takes time in the forest, and in his final phase becomes the transformed and emancipated elder.

We can value this tradition for its emphasis on the need for time set apart to seek a deeper union with the Divine. As we enter the twenty-first century, however, we recognize the fluid and unpredictable nature of our contemporary lives. It is, therefore, all the more important to honor forest time as one of the necessary rhythms which helps us to keep our balance as we move through our individual life cycles.

The quality of time in the forest is different for those who have grown up in the last half-century. As one man said, "We were schooled in thinking that you leave one thing to go to another." Travel has been purposeful and linear. Plans were made: First a, then b, then c. Upward movement was fueled by our desire to succeed. The driving question was: How can I *get there?*

In contrast to measurable upward and onward mobility, forest time is experienced as process. For some of us, it takes us through the darkness of not knowing. Different from the quieting darkness that welcomes us, this kind of darkness forces us to confront our-selves in the midst of unknown territory. The important question becomes not so much "How can I get *there?*" as it is "How can I be right *here* where I am?"

For us as Westerners this is one of the hardest things to do. One of the gifts from Eastern religious traditions is the practice of meditation. For centuries, Buddhists and Christian contemplatives have practiced ways to be present, ways to let thoughts come and go. Thich Nhat Hanh offers the way of mindfulness. Christian meditation practice points to the use of a mantra or a breath prayer. Both focus on our breath, which is always available to recall us to be right here, now (see chap. 6).

Sometimes "here" means being present to my sadness, confusion, desire to run away; my fear, anxiety, or remorse. These become "openings for soul," as Thomas Moore has said. When we allow ourselves to go deeper and become familiar with these experiences, we form our individuality. Soul often "appears in places where we are unsuccessful. . . . Our lives are shaped around the gaps and holes."[50] How different this is from the typical Western success story so often told as a movement away from these empty spaces.

At a time when it looked as if this writing project was not going to work or ever come to fruition, I felt forced into the forest. Painfully I tried to keep walking through my days. I felt as if the light on my path had been shut off. Questions came at me from that darkness. What will come of these years of writing? What am I doing now, anyway? What is the purpose of all this soul work? How can I keep going when I don't know where I'll come out?

I finally went to a nearby monastery for a twenty-four-hour retreat. My time there felt like the wilderness, even though it was a familiar place and has been sacred space for me over the years. I wrote in my journal, dating the entry: DAY BEFORE ASH WEDNESDAY.

One more circle down through the familiar of the clutching, grasping hand. The fear of non-being, the holding on so tight to the known, because of the emptiness. Fears like being unknown, all on my own, without support—alone— left alone. My point of separation from God, this place of deepest fear.

Holding on for dear life—for life! I will not let go. Yet, ironically, my grasp leaves no space for life, for Spirit, for fire, for God. I am holding on to survive but not to live.

In *Crossing to Avalon*, Jean Shinoda Bolen, M.D., writes as a traveler who had "awakened to find herself in a dark wood." This forest time began in the midst of her householding years.

> We find ourselves "in the forest" when we have lost our usual bearings; when we find ourselves questioning the meaning of what we are doing or who we are with, or have serious doubts about the path we have followed or the turn we took at the last crossroads.... The inability for life to go on as usual comes about for any number of reasons. It is not the event itself that does it but the depth into which our souls go as a result.[51]

Several years ago I became acquainted with a woman whose faith as a Quaker is core to her being. With the slow onset of multiple sclerosis, her soul was forced to go into a depth which became a place of learning for her.

> When I feel that my plans have been diverted, scuttled, or I have felt the dark night of the soul, it is a time when I feel I don't want to be here. Yet I am so glad I that I am. It is totally against what I will, wish, or would like to happen, but I am learning so much from being here not only in the mental state but learning in the heart condition.

She told me that she is no longer spending time thinking about what she used to be able to do, grieving that loss, but she tries to focus on "what is present to me now." She remembers and cherishes what was, as memory, but is not longing for it now, choosing instead to put energy into her present situation. In many ways she is living out the vow of stability while being in the midst of impermanence.

I think people who have been really identified with their job, getting their sense of self-worth from it and then lose it, are faced with this same thing. If we have not developed an inner connection we keep holding on to what was externally. It's the same with aging. Family members say: I remember you when. . . . That doesn't help. What is important is now and the inner condition.

Many of us are challenged to tend our inner condition by being forced to "downsize" or "re-invent"; to adjust our lifestyle and our way of measuring success. My Quaker friend finds that the words of Saint Teresa of Avila provide strength and comfort: "The Lord does not look so much at the magnitude of anything we do but at the love with which we do it." These words encourage her as she seeks to be fully present in her inner heart condition while the outer conditions continue to change. The essence of her challenge comes to all of us in different ways. Though our experience differs, the core truth is touched in Meister Eckhart's words: "God is not found by adding any thing but by a process of subtraction."[52]

In the forest, growth does comes out of "the process of subtraction." The great fires of Yellowstone National Park burned through 160,000 acres in the summer of 1988. The policy for woodland fire management at that time gave discretion to park officials in handling fires ignited by natural forces. They were monitored each day and allowed to burn if they did not threaten life or property.

Their policy was based on the idea that naturally ignited fires do "a number of important jobs in tending forests and making meadows." They actually "promote re-growth of diverse vegetation," which in turn supports new animal life. They clean out "deadfall" or old kindling and finally create new passageways "through and around expanses of otherwise solid forest, thereby reducing the risk of catastrophic fire spread."[53]

The cleaning out process that happens in the natural world of the forest also happens in our soul work. We may not choose the circumstances that force us to growth by subtraction, but we can choose to move with this rhythm that clears out space and opens up possibility for our inner life. When we consciously spend time in the forest, we become more authentically who we are.

Our culture does not support us in this particular rhythm. Unlike the Hindu culture, our Western world offers no encouragement for solitude for women or men. Children's lives are being programmed as much or more than adults. Time apart without agenda is rare. Therefore, we must encourage one another to make time for this balancing rhythm. It is so easy to let the needs of others and our need for connection override our need for time apart. A businesswoman named her need clearly:

> It seems that life lately has caused me to stretch in ways that seem to squeeze out any cushion or margin of protection that the healing power of reflection provides. I literally have not been able to find where I can go for peace and stillness and just be or think or savor the weaving together of new

experiences. There is no joy in growth or new frontiers when there is no balancing time and space to notice the context in which I live, work, breathe, sleep, eat, and interact. I feel like a horse with blinders, nose to the grindstone. How can I slow down the pace?

"We need to be ruthless," one woman said. I did not like the sound of that word. However, one of its meanings is: without sorrow or regret. A contemplative nun put it this way: "Be draconian." That, too, is surprisingly strong encouragement to the contemplative within each of us to be forceful about creating time apart, and then to be protective of it once you have set it aside.

A woman whose children are now established in careers on the West Coast lives alone. She decided to physically move away from her well known "life in the village," her apartment home of seven years, which was in the center of town. She became aware of her need to reconnect with the center of her self and felt pulled away from that process by the activity of her life.

Her journey of only a few miles to a more secluded apartment became a pilgrimage. "A journey becomes a pilgrimage when we are consciously engaged in going to a center, deliberately going into the center with the purpose of going to the sacred center."[54]

In retrospect, I have become aware that I was in a forest time of my life. I had wanted a bit more isolation. From years of over-involvement and over-choosing, my body was asking for time out. It took a while for me to get the message. Finally, several friends spoke to me and I listened to their wise words. Slowly, reluctantly, I gave up one activity after another. The relief was palpable. I now wonder how I kept such a rigorous schedule and . . . why?

In this process, which became a form of growth by subtraction, she learned from her solitude that she "must constantly step back and choose more wisely as to where to put time and attention."

> This calls for constant vigilance and assessment, for life is constantly pulsing, pulling, offering. Time apart is essential to my well-being, otherwise I become blurred, my ability to be inner-directed is dulled. Being alone, being quiet allows me to hear that still small voice within, which I choose to believe is the universal life force within all and beyond all— the unknowable, whom some call God.

Time in the Western world is most often thought of as linear. We ask, how long does it take? In the forest experience, time has to do with the depth dimension. It cannot be measured by its length. The quality of the time is what gives it value. This is very helpful for us to recognize as women who for the most part will not be able to leave our householding situations for an extended period of time. We can, however, find ways to consciously choose forest time. If the essence of forest time is solitude and a choice to be fully present and available for soul work, then we can create forest time anywhere.

A mother of school-aged children returned to school herself. As a student caught up in the fire of that focused time, she was also aware of her need for silence as a balancing rhythm. She was able to name her need and claim it.

> The most important piece keeping me on my path is my "time in the forest." I drive forty minutes each way to school. I get into my car early in the morning and usually listen to the radio for the first ten minutes. Then I begin to crave silence and my time with God.

I specifically remember one occasion when I was questioning my path. My self-doubt was clouding my ability to feel God's presence. I decided to trust God with my feelings. And as I crossed the bridge at 7:15 A.M. on this dreary January morning, a surreal, bright, life-giving ray of sun shone through the gray sky. I glanced at the hurried drivers around me and realized that this was my gift from God, my connection, the light on my path.

One of my biggest fears about returning to school was how much I would dread the commute. The time in my car, with no phone, no TV, no computer, no kids, has become my time apart. God is my constant companion. I am very protective of this time.

We each have to name our need and claim our form of forest time. It can take place during an extended time apart or during a daily ritual such as driving to school, waiting for a bus, sitting on a train, swimming laps, peeling potatoes, or taking a morning walk. The choice for solitude and the intention of openness and availability can take us there.

Reflection

1. The words "assimilation, distillation, and integration" may not describe your experience of time in the forest. What words or images fit your experience?

2. Has spiritual growth by subtraction been a part of your forest time? If so, take time to recall what it was like for you.

DIFFERENT PATHS

There are many different paths into the forest. What is most important is to become aware of where we are and begin there.

We may not be able to choose the path that we follow. Some of us find ourselves on the way into the forest before we realize that we have started on the path. We can, however, choose to walk our particular path with awareness.

> I have this fantasy of going to the airport, and standing under the board that tells the destinations of the flights that are departing. I look up and when I see a place that looks good to me, I say: I think I'll go to... Spain. And I get on the plane and go.

This longing was expressed by a man who at fifty "became an orphan and a grandfather." He had cared for dying parents and seen his son's son born within the same year. He was longing for time without a schedule, non-agenda time; time to listen and be open to what he might do next. He asked, "Is it possible to go into the forest while living the householder's life? I tend to think of it in all-or-nothing terms." Owning our longings is the first step in awareness and in honoring our need for time apart.

One woman's life changed at fifty with the need for her to take up full-time work in the city. Her day now begins very early and ends late due to her hour-and-a-half commute. As an introvert, one who is recharged and replenished by time alone, she longs for solitude.

> I do have a bent toward introversion and *am* restored by having time alone, by moments of stillness. One small "window of opportunity" I have is the ride on the train each weekday. It is a fairly private time. I often have my own "compartment." I may look out the window, doze, read, write, or meditate ... a sense of beauty is missing ... a sense of stillness is not there ... but it is more peaceful than the day's activity.

We need to begin where we are and not wait until our circumstances change. Most often we make entry into the forest on a path that originates in our everyday life.

A young mother speaks of her own body as her way into time apart. The natural rhythm that so many women feel in the days leading up to our menstrual flow is a pull toward an inward time, she calls it "cave time," which translates: curl-up-in-the-bed-and-read time. If we listened to our body's call, we would simply say: "I want to be alone," so difficult for women to do, especially mothers and other caretakers.

Ancient traditions supported women in their need for time apart during their menstrual cycles. Today we need to do that for each other. This young mother, who is most often energized by being with people, was encouraged when a friend said to her, "You have to learn how to name this need and claim it." Whether we are thirty or fifty, this is our challenge. This is where we begin.

There are those of us who are more extroverted, who would say, as did one sixty-year-old woman: "I am not sure of what I think until I say it." The way into the forest for an extrovert, one who is energized by being in contact with other people, may not be obvious at first, as this same woman reflected:

> I believe I have achieved a good amount of assimilation, distillation, and integration as I have lived out my life. But I am not conscious of taking the time apart to make this happen. My time for reflection most often occurs in the midst of the mundane: ironing clothes, housework, driving the car, and most especially in the shower, which is also the venue for much of my mental creative work: ideas are born and often fleshed out there.
>
> I think of myself as a hunter/gatherer (another word might be seeker) by nature. Perhaps I would be well served to say "enough" and check out some forest time for the purpose of integrating what has been gathered. This is worth exploring.

Whether we naturally tend toward extraversion or introversion, we each have our own particular need for time to assimilate, distill, and integrate our life experience. Our ways to meet this need will be different.

There is also variation in our experience of the literal forest. For some of us it is a welcoming place. The woods hold wonderful childhood memories and we choose to go into it to recover ourselves. This is true for an artistic woman in her forties who now lives a very different life than she did as an engineer who commuted daily up and down Route 128 and "thought everyone did that." But not every engineer walked at lunch hour as a way to ground herself and connect with the earth. Following her walk she wrote in her journal, a resource that has been with her since second grade when she used it "to talk to myself."

Now, as an adult traveling an unfamiliar path as she tries to become pregnant through a sperm donor, she uses her journal as a way of "being with the unknowns. I talk with others, especially my partner, but my journal is always there for me, helping me bounce thoughts and bringing me deeper."

> I thread my way through this process of trying to become pregnant, honoring my inner voice and my longing to be mother to a child. When I get caught up in the questions and the doubts, walking helps me to change my focus....
>
> The woods were where I went for nurturing as a child. They were always there, a place that accepted me. I could be who I was. They were nonjudgmental, always ready to embrace me. For me the woods were safe and trustworthy.
>
> Now when I am in unknown places or situations, I turn to familiars, a rock, a shell, a feather. They are signs of things I've had for years. I don't feel lonely when they surround me. I have friends. When I travel, I carry familiars with me as touchstones. They are part of a bigger entity, the earth. They remind me that wherever I am my feet can walk the earth every day. Mother Earth embraces me wherever I am. I am not separate or disconnected; I am part of the whole.

The woods have not been nurturing for others. One woman remembers that when she was "growing up, having bugs and creeping things in our house was a sign of uncleanness and felt threatening to me as a child. The woods seemed to be full of just those things and a place to stay away from." The forest can be a frightening place or a symbolic place of the unknown—"the dark wood" as Dante called it. Jean Bolen refers to the dark wood as the place "where we go when we are lost, and it is where we need to go in order to find ourselves."[55] Kathleen Norris speaks of this experience in her poem "The Companionable Dark."

> Not the easy dark
> of dusk and candles,
> but the dark from which comforts flee.
> The deep down dark
> of one by one,
> dark of wind
> and dust, dark in which stars burn.[56]

As we consider the various circumstances that can lead us into the life rhythm of time apart, it is important for each person to recognize and use imagery and metaphors that fit her own experience. In many spiritual traditions, the desert has been used as the counterpart to civilization and the life of community. For centuries the desert has been a place to which many men and women go to simplify their lives, reconnect with their essential natures, and be opened up to the holy. A woman who lives in New England discovered this for herself.

> For me the desert is a place of solitude and spiritual renewal. It is a welcoming place, a quiet elemental place of dry starkness, a place where my inner defenses and outer pretenses fall away—a place to rest. This land of spaciousness is a "thin" place for me, where I can reconnect with my inner silent center, God, my true being.
>
> Yet the desert is also full of life and a place of surprising abundance. Vegetation has learned to survive and I learn from its wisdom. During a deluge the saguaro cactus can expand and store water in a spongy layer, then draw on it in times of drought. I, too, store up spiritual nourishment and richness during my desert times, drawing on this inner reservoir when I return to my life of constantly attending to others' needs as a teacher, friend, and family member.

Both the forest and the desert can also feel like wilderness. "They become wilderness when I feel lost," one woman said. Both provide a metaphor for the unknown territory in which we find ourselves, having come there by a route that we did not choose. Sometimes we may spend days, months in the wilderness. Wilderness can also be a moment in time. Beverly Williams describes this.

> Wilderness moments might be filled
> with new and unknown events.
> Breathtaking fears may freeze me
> like a deer's eyes
> in headlights.
>
> Breath/prayers break the spell
> allow the spirit back in,
> allow the tense muscles ease and release.
>
> Wilderness time may be space and time
> stretched far ahead into black darkness.
> I gaze ahead
> without knowledge
> of what is held in that deep dark.
> Breath/prayers turn black into a soft velvet cloak
> spread out before me like an offering.
>
> Wilderness time is a crack in the earth
> an eruption that throws you down
> where you fall and fall deep.
> But grace can come at those times.
> The grace of a friend or a counselor
> to help you regain your footing
> or light the way in their bright love and caring.

And then I have gained a new depth to my soul.
I have connected with the sages and saints,
the wise men and wise crones.
I look at the world with more tenderness
and more forgiveness.

Stepping out of the wilderness,
my power has grown and my forgiving
can include myself.[57]

Another thoughtful woman reflected on her experience of the wilderness and called that "time in the desert."

One is driven into the desert. It is arid there, first hot then cold, lifeless until torrential rains force cactus blooms and wash away gophers' homes. It is a place of deep transformation, but it is unpredictable, barren, and hostile. It has been the desert, not the forest, that I have experienced when I have lost my bearings or had serious questions about my life.... Sometimes great desert storms have swept me into a dramatic job change or even a whole career switch.

We experience the wilderness aspect of this rhythm of solitude by traveling through the unknown, be it named the desert, the dark wood, a voyage over vast ocean in a small boat, or other metaphors that describe a journey through unfamiliar territory. One woman described being in a small boat at sea as being "cast into wilderness" where there are "no outside supports, affirmations, resources."

In the wilderness with no things, we are at great risk of "nothingness." It feels a powerful, powerless place. There are depths of self and God to be known which require a stripped bare agony of loneliness that is not named in forest gardens. Wilderness is a time to be wary of as well as time to be embraced.

Those who travel uncharted journeys share the common need to assimilate our life experiences and to live from our own depths in an authentic way. This need leads some people into what they would call a journey of descent, which is another form of travel through the wilderness into the unknown. A woman shared the story of her "deeper journey" with me.

> What I didn't recognize until after the fact, is that you go into the forest ALONE. When I knew about the incest, in that second, my life changed upside down, and it was just the beginning of the journey, the deeper journey. It would mean I'd have to change everything, or more accurately everything would have to change in me—it would have to happen. The truth was there, but hidden. I was seeing the wrong picture for fifty years, and then I saw the truth in an instant—the beginning of forest time for me because of the knowing.

For this woman in her fifties the journey was a descent into the unconscious in order to bring truth into the light of consciousness. "And the descent has to be made alone!"

> Many times I thought I was alone, and I wasn't. My body was alone, but I was attached to the old ways, unconsciously— and that had to break apart, leaving me for a while with nothing but life itself. I was alive!
>
> Going alone. Changing. Losing everything, or so I thought. I lost my old mind structure, deeply. I lost my

family in the way I conceived of them. I loved them! And I can love them now. But in between—I had to pass through the unspeakable, the hidden, and the cover-up. The betrayal! And only now am I learning that it is universal, not only my private problem.

Forest time. Frightening! Why do it? In fairy tales, many get forced into the forest by circumstances, as I did by having memories. I could not tell people about my time in the forest until after I got out.

As a way to return, she began to tell nursery rhymes and stories to young children. Along with working on her own story she finds that this is a way to assimilate all that has happened. Forest time continues to be "essential" for her.

The way into the forest changes at different times in our lives. The woman who eventually became a storyteller needed a prolonged time in the forest during which her unconscious attachment to "the old ways" had to "break apart." She had to go through the shattering of the "old mind structure" before she could begin to assimilate, distill, and integrate her experience. Today she lives "at the edge of the forest," where she can go in and come out as she chooses in order to continue this personal work. She finds her own rhythm for time apart and then returns to her life "in the village" with young children, friends, and family.

Our journeys in and out of the forest are unique to each one of us. We need to travel alone to reach the center of the forest. When we return and share our experience of this journey, we connect more deeply with other pilgrims.

Clustering Exercise: Adapted for Journal Writing

This "clustering" exercise may be helpful in your reflection on forest time. It was developed and is creatively applied by Dr. Gabriel Lusser Rico in *Writing the Natural Way.*[58]

Objective: To stimulate intuitive writing in prose or poetry and to deepen your understanding of forest time.

Time: Twenty to thirty minutes.

Materials needed: Journal, pen or pencil; quiet space.

Procedure:

1. In the center of an empty journal page, place the word (in this case a phrase, forest time) that you want to explore. Put a small circle around it.

2. Then allow words to come that you associate with forest time. Circle each word and connect it with a line to the previous word.

Continue with that line until you run out of words. Then go back to the central word, forest time, and start again with a new association of words. Keep going like this until you have exhausted the possibilities. It may look something like this.

3. When you have finished clustering, turn to a new page in your journal. The words will stay with you, they have primed the pump to let your words flow now. Write freely of your experience of forest time.

18

SACRED INTENT

At the center of the forest is a deep pool. It is called solitude. We get to it by many paths. Solitude is the inner and outer place where I rest in God, where I finally let God be God and I let go.

"Be still and know that I am God" (Psalm 46) especially speaks to me when I see and hear it in this way.

> Be still and know that I am God.
> Be still and know that I am.
> Be still and know.
> Be still.
> Be.

These wonderful words touch the deep longing in many of us to rest our souls in God. Yet our lives seem to allow little opportunity to get to that centered place of solitude and stillness.

"Centering down" brings Quakers to that place of stillness where "our body and our mind are in the same place."[59] When we are able to "be still and cool" in our own minds and hearts, as George Fox encouraged the early Friends, we move toward our own center. In the words of Sister Donald Corcoran,

> At our own center we find the Center of all centers—Infinite Loving Mystery—that, far from isolating us, brings us to

our true communion with others and with God. Our life is wholed, harmonized, integrated, "con-centrated"—enriched even as it is simplified.[60]

The way of traveling toward our center is different for each of us, but when we seek solitude it often is like a pilgrimage to find that pool at the center of the forest. It lies in the heart of the forest. It is also at the heart of each one of us. And so we long for it. "As a deer longs for flowing streams, so my soul longs for you, O God" (Psalm 42:1).

> Solitude calls to me powerfully. At this life juncture my daily schedule means: rise at 5 A.M., leave home at 6, work, then arrive home at 7 P.M. Dinner and dishes take me to 8 P.M. The next hour is available for phone calls, chores, a meeting or a visit with a friend, reading. Weekends include shopping, activities, etc. It is something of a treadmill, compelling me to push, push, push to fit it all in and do it well.
>
> Time for restoration is not abundant: yoga, meditation, retreat silence, fun, play, extended time to focus on the soul's needs seem limited to me. So forest time does call to me— powerfully. And the call is not adequately filled....
>
> I thirst...I want more of it.
>
> I am reminded of the twenty-third psalm...he maketh me to lie down in green pastures...he leadeth me beside still waters...he restoreth my soul.

This woman expresses her thirst for solitude. Naming it is like holding a compass in her hand, being guided as she walks through her day. Her longing is like magnetic north reminding her that she is on a pilgrimage toward the center. Her yearning for forest time heightens her awareness, so that she can claim moments that restore her soul: "planting and caring for the garden, bringing flowers to bloom and being outside. Cooking and feeling that is nurturing, I feel joy in sensing appreciation for good food." Her list goes on.

Her dream life also guides her. She recognized that dreams are gifts created in the solitude of night's darkness and can feed our souls. She had a dream that took place at the edge of the forest. In it she is with a young woman who will not leave the rich forest life and its creatures. In working with this dream, she realized that the woods have always been a place that she has loved and trusted: a true place of replenishment. In her dreams, the images from the woods are in stark contrast to those from her work scene. The contrast gets her attention. She is drawn now to attend to these images and let them lead her toward the center. As a biologist and an artist, she wants to learn more about forest life. Excited about what may unfold in her exploration, she also asks herself: How can I carry the qualities of this sacred space in my dream to replenish me while I am in my work world?

Water seems to be a common image for those who seek replenishment in solitude. Like the pool at the center of the forest, we are drawn toward a place where we can "simply be," as one woman said, "to rest, restore, and renew—a soul-resting time." A fifty-year-old woman was wrestling with a decision about her life work, and sought this kind of "soul resting" by the water in a day of personal retreat at our home. With her journal and a few books she set off for the Headlands. She later described how she made her way closer and closer to the water. Shedding her books, she left them in a pile on the rocks. Feeling the need to get as close to the water as she could, she left her journal in another place. "I needed to get down close to the water and just be there with nothing in my hands: no agenda—only to be with the water and to be open."

A young mother also seeks the replenishment of being near the water.

> Sometimes I just need to tell my husband that I am going running! I'll be back. Goodbye! Instead of waiting for him to say "Why don't you...," wanting him to recognize my need—my lack of solitude—my need to be alone in my own house without my family. It would be easier if he anticipated my need, but he can't always do that. So I have to. I know I'll be better and they will feel better with me if I do it. I run in the park. Alone, not with a friend. I run through the old growth trees and by the water. Water is grounding for me. The vastness of the water forces me to breathe deeply. That is what draws me there.

A woman in midlife walks to view an "ancient creek" which flows through the town where she lives. "I think of its power as it moves the leaves down the stream at this time of year. Also I see gentleness in this water as well." In her life and work as a consultant, this balance of power and gentleness is crucial.

> Also as I drive to see my clients along the Schuylkill River, I have begun to gaze more and more at the water. The water is helping me to slow down my ever moving mind, to try to breathe deep and think more clearly.

"To either be in water when I swim or by water when I walk, helps me take back my energy," says a writer who has a young child. I read the very same sentiment in my own journal: "I need to gather my energy into the center. To focus. I feel so many pulls." And so I head for the beach. In my ritual of returning to the water, I also draw on the resources that restore my soul.

As I approach the small beach at low tide, the smell of sea weed, churned up and strewn by the recent storm, reaches me. When I last walked here, only days ago, sand covered the beach. Today that smooth blanket is gone. It was taken out by the storm, and now large and small stones remain, making passage to the water's edge a concentrated effort. Once again I am reminded of life's impermanence by this familiar yet always changing beach.

I make my way across the stones to the smooth sand near the incoming waves. Half closing my eyes to better hear the rolling rhythm, I walk back and forth, breathing in and breathing out the smells, the sounds, the moisture in the air. My footsteps move into walking meditation as I open myself to become a space to receive what I need.

This beach has been a welcoming place for me in times of pain and in times of fullness. I bring my heart's concerns here, my tears, my struggles, my questions, and my prayers. To this place of letting go into vastness, sky and water, I seem to be able, if only for moments, to surrender my attempts at control.

I think of my friend who comes here with her dog later in the morning. This place offers her solitude. I know that she has often prayed for me and for my loved ones on this beach. While her dog fetches sticks, she writes names in the sand. As she writes each name she prays for the person, offering her concerns to God until the water takes the name away.

Today the storm has left a gift for me. A large low block of granite is uncovered once again. A year ago I came upon this rock that bares a pattern of two-inch marks along its edge, a reject perhaps from the days of quarrying at the beginning of this century. For me its hollowed-out center space creates a font of holy water. Leaning down, I dip two fingers into the cold, clear water. Touching my forehead I begin in slow motion to make the sign of the cross.

This ritual is not familiar to my American Protestant heritage, but has come to hold deep meaning for me. In this movement, I acknowledge my concerns, my loved ones, and myself within the fourfold reality of the providence of God, the presence of Christ, the life of the Spirit, and the openness of Mary. These words have come from the living of my days, each phrase crafted in the fire of my struggles and my longings. In the tradition of my Celtic forebears, I use them as a journey blessing. It is part of my daily ritual.

When I say the words, I ground myself in these affirmations of faith which enable me to walk the path that is mine. As I touch myself with the water, I am awakened by the cold fresh reminder: to trust in One whose wisdom and purpose are beyond my understanding, to walk with a knowledge that I dwell within a presence that is available step-by-step along the way, to acknowledge the creative energy of God at work in our world and in me as I open my self to be available to that Spirit.

Turning back to walk the beach, I reach into my pocket for a verse that speaks to my condition of the moment—just enough words to fill the back of my business card. Looking to this cue card, which fits in the palm of my hand, I repeat the phrases over and over in the meter of my stride. Body, mind, and spirit come together in this repetition. O God, "you have searched me and known me. You know when I sit down and when I rise up; you discern my thoughts from far away" (Psalm 139:1).

I think of nuns and monks, who for centuries have paced the cloisters of monasteries all over the world, repeating ancient, sacred words with the rhythm of their steps. I join them now in my walking. It is grounding for me as I anticipate my day with its concerns and commitments. Walking with a psalm helps me to focus and connects me with the contemplative tradition that seeks to live from the center in both solitude and community.

When the wind is right the sound of the steeple bell can be heard, telling me the hour. It is hard to leave. I turn from the waves' rhythm and the smell of the sea. Breathing in and breathing out, I remember that I carry within me the same rhythm.

> Breathing in and breathing out
> waves roll in and waves roll out
> tide comes in, tide goes out
> the sand leaves, the sand returns
> seasons come, seasons go
> the space remains.

I turn toward home. Depending on time and whim, I retrace my steps or take another route. I play with time: long route, short route? I decide which garden to look at, which dog to greet or avoid. It is fun deciding which road to take. Today my walk has been longer than usual; I will take the short route. Thoughts of the day ahead begin to come. As I pass by certain houses I think of the stories within. There seems to be space now for these thoughts and often a prayer, the beach's gift to me.

Retreats are a gift when solitude is supported and permission is in the environment of a retreat center to "be still and know that I am God." A single mother of three daughters speaks from her rare and treasured experience of time in the forest when she is on retreat.

For me there are layers in forest time. At first I am shedding off the busyness of getting there to my place of retreat.

I am letting go of all the arrangements and details of my journey, the things left undone, the children and work left behind.... As I let those things go, I sink deeper.

Beginning to notice the stillness and beauty all around me, I become more present, quieter, sinking into yet another layer, into that peaceful place where there are no interruptions.... I am present to my own inner voice and strength.

After a few days I feel almost a floating sensation ... adrift in quiet—able to hear my own inner workings as well as the myriad sounds of nature. Just as I am settling into this deeper place of being as opposed to doing, it is time to pick up and go back to my life.

The transition, returning to life in the village, is an important part of the retreat, often difficult. It takes some planning and preparation for the return; for example, bringing back familiars from the time of retreat to re-call oneself to the time of "being" in the stillness.

A "quiet day" is another opportunity for solitude while we are in the village. This event is offered for several hours in a church or place of gathering where silence is guided by a leader and maintained by the participants. A woman described her first experience of this kind of solitude in community.

At first there was the usual jitters about being with new people and not knowing what to expect—except that it was to be a silent retreat day and I would not have to talk. More importantly, no one else would be talking either, which would allow me to be with myself and to stay with myself.

Some people create times of solitude as part of their weekly schedule. "I set up one day a week," said an artist, "and I frame it in silence." When we hold the intention for forest time, we can then seize the moment when it presents itself. "I recently discovered forest time happens after going to bed when I reflect back on the day," says a musician. In her daytime hours she is also conscious of the quality of forest time that she experiences while practicing the organ for two hours.

> Practicing a musical instrument for me is an active meditation. There is a focus, feeling beyond words, activity with a quiet center. I may be tired afterward but almost always feel refreshed and centered.

A "time of sacred intent," as one woman named it, recalls us to our sense of pilgrimage toward the center of our own being and the Center of all centers, both of which lie deep at the heart of forest time. "More and more I seem to be choosing time apart and feel extremely fortunate to have it," says a grandmother.

> This is the time in my life when I see the daughters of my daughters, though I don't plan to leave family and possessions and go into the forest to live as a hermit. What is important to me is to have the right balance of time alone and time with others.

Whenever and however we take time apart to dip into the waters of solitude and silence, we are replenished and our store of living water increases. For this reason it is essential that we hold this "sacred intent," whatever our age, whatever our circumstance.

Reflection

1. Remember a time in solitude which replenished your soul. As you do this, consider the four elements: water, earth, fire, and air. Which of these elements was present in your time of solitude?

2. In your times of solitude now, be aware of these four elements. Consider how you could include one or more of them in a simple ritual that recalls you to your sacred intent.

19

HOLY MOMENTS

It is Lent. I have not been able to realize my intention to have time apart in solitude except in small segments. My longing for extended time in the forest remains: time to walk familiar paths and reflect as I wander, to feel no agenda but being present, to find a place of rest where I can replenish my soul.

During these forty days I have felt that I, too, have been driven into a harsh wilderness area rather than being led beside still waters. It has been a period of facing hard situations in relationships, confronting death and other losses, coming to terms with parts of myself that force me to continue to grow. This path through the wilderness was not what I imagined when I made a commitment to deepen my union with God. Give me a moss-covered glen at the heart of the forest—that's where I want to be.

And now it is Holy Week, a week of events in the journey with Jesus when I make myself available to the Spirit within the momentum of these days. What makes this hard time "holy"? A nine-year-old once asked me: "What's so holy about what happened to Jesus? His friends told on him and left him alone and he died on a cross."

It is just as hard at fifty-nine to apprehend the presence of the Holy One in the midst of loneliness, suffering, and death. Yet the message of the incarnation continues to confront me: God is with us, in the flesh, here, now, in our midst. Each year I go deeper with this good news that is integral to the Holy Week experience. Holy events in my tradition help me to recognize holy events in my own life, events that bring me closer to the heart of the mystery at the center of the Christian faith.

It is hard to describe experiences that can be called holy events or holy moments. Many times, I have wanted to stop trying to do that and simply live my way into the mystery that I touch at those times. I return to the words of Gabriel Marcel, words which spoke to me many years ago.

> Wherever one is involved in mystery, one is involved as a total person in an intimate set of relations which can never be grasped as something apart from one's self and held up as an object of knowledge. The recognition of mystery is a function of the whole person and is as much a matter of living one's self into the heart of mystery as of thinking.[61]

Holy events occur in the midst of our daily life when we are open to or driven to engage the sacred with our soul entire, our whole self. We live our way in.

In my recent wilderness time, I discovered the words of Diogenes Allen. In his book *Temptation* he makes a distinction between problems and mysteries.

> For we do not solve mysteries; we enter into them. The deeper we enter into them, the more illumination we get. Still greater depths are revealed to us the further we go . . . a mystery once recognized is something we are never finished with. It is never exhausted. Instead we return to it again and again and it unfolds new levels to us.[62]

Holy events are not always recognizable at first. Sometimes we are headed for what we think is what we need and we are given the opportunity to go to "greater depths" by a different route. This was my experience when I made my private retreat at Kirkridge several years ago. I went anticipating an undisturbed place of rest and replenishment.

My first day in the cottage by the side of the road was a let-down day. My body desperately needed just that. I moved slowly through the morning, becoming familiar with the three rooms of the cottage. At breakfast, I sat for a long time at the table looking out into the wooded hills before me. I found an old lounge chair and wrapped myself in a blanket to lie out under a large tree and listen to the birds who had claimed the day as their own. I had no claims on the day, no agenda but to begin to open myself to the solitude that I had finally chosen.

By afternoon I was ready to venture forth. In a ritual of returning, I went to a cleared field at the foot of the forest trails which led up the mountain. Years ago I came to this meadow alone in the darkness to enact a dream vision as part of a workshop on dreams. That night, with a staff in my hand, I walked a spiral path, moving from the perimeter around and around to the center and back. In the darkness I repeated the twenty-third psalm over and over as I walked. Years later, in the afternoon light, I repeated the path and the psalm. I remembered with my body the sense of strength, courage, and trust that I felt that night years ago when I walked at the edge of the forest.

I returned to the cottage at the end of the day. Sleep lured me. Sometime during the night, I woke myself from a dream— shouting for help. Twice I called out. Heart pounding with fear, I lay there with the images of my dream. I wrote them down on the pad of paper beside my bed.

An attractive young nurse is taking care of an elderly person. The nurse has taken a fancy to me. At some point I am drawn to help someone who needs me. The nurse becomes rabidly jealous and comes at me with a hypodermic needle. She injects me in the elbow. I begin to lose consciousness. I cry out: Help me! Help me!

Unable to return to sleep, I warmed some milk and sat at the table. As a way to clear myself to return to sleep, I used my journal to review where I had been in the preceding two weeks. It was the horrific memories of the Holocaust Museum that kept surfacing. A week earlier, I had spent several hours there by myself but had not taken the necessary time to process what I experienced.

When I am awakened in the night abruptly, it is often because I have not tended my soul's needs. It became obvious to me from my dream that I was still being profoundly affected by my direct and powerful encounter with evil at the museum. No longer on the move, I could finally assimilate that experience and my own fears that were aroused. It took a nightmare to get my attention. Later in my retreat, I reflected in my journal on this gift from my unconscious.

I have not had a powerful dream like this for a long time. I sense that I needed this very much to clear out the space— blast it out—blow it out with the force of the wind of the Spirit from the stimulation of the last two weeks. There has been so much to take in!

In my reading I had been savoring Allan Chinen's book on fairy tales and the second half of life called *In the Ever After.* I was aware of synchronicity as I sat in the cottage reading tales and commentary about elders who chose to live "at the edge of the forest." According to Chinen, "the marginal location symbolizes the boundary between conscious and unconscious, and reflects a central theme in elder tales: confronting neglected aspects of our self, hidden in the unconscious."[63]

Chinen also reminds the reader that "confronting one's own evil is a major task of maturity."[64] This was not at all what I had planned to do as I settled into this cottage at the edge of the forest for my retreat time. Yet I do believe that I am not given a dream by my deep self unless I am ready for it. Encouraged by Chinen's knowledge of adult development and his sensitivity to the journey of the second half of life, I accepted the challenge from my deep self, which was expressed in my dream. I needed to help myself wake up!

Puns in a dream are always helpful. They do get my attention. It was time to deal with the part of me that *nurses* my need to be number one, the one and only. Jealousy is familiar to me as a first child in my family of origin. It can become rabid when I unconsciously *inject* it into my current life. It becomes my "own evil" as Chinen names it, for jealousy can consume my energy and affect all my relationships. My dream was warning me that I was losing consciousness again about this part of myself. It was time to bring the jealous one into the light. And so the agenda for my retreat unfolded.

While doing my inner work, I also made it a point to become familiar with the world outside me. I recorded what I observed and wrote simple poems in the little journal that I carry in my pocket. In my daily routine in the cottage I returned to the rituals that sustain and support me.

I think back now to that wilderness time and recognize that it was a holy event in my life. My spiritual practice was deepened and distilled in those days. Without knowing it then, I was drawing

on the Benedictine vows that since have become more and more
a part of my life.

STABILITY: I tried to stay with the difficult material that came to
my consciousness through dreamwork, meditation, walking with
the twenty-third psalm, and repeating it with the rhythm of my
steps as I daily explored the paths leading from the forest's edge.

OPENNESS TO CHANGE: I had further letting go to do. Jealousy
has been a companion of mine for many years. It can fester and
be very destructive and is a real threat to my conscious choosing.
It can become evil when it threatens fullness of life.

LISTENING TO THE HOLY ONE: I listened as I walked through
the glories of creation. I also needed to be still and available to
the leading of the Spirit in motionless silence. I sought healing
and forgiveness. I asked God for help.

I created my own fourth vow: PLAY. This new vow becomes
more and more important to me as I approach my elder years. I
played with water colors and collage, experimenting with texture
and shape. Now, as I re-read my journal, I find a fairy tale which I
wrote the day before I left Kirkridge. My fairy tale connected me
to a quality that has been emerging in me since that time in the
forest, affecting my family life and my work in the village.

Holy events happen over time. There are also holy moments
in which it is possible to have a brief encounter with mystery
that then continues to unfold over a lifetime. In my last years
at college, the chapel on the hill became a home. It was the late
fifties and the energy of the sixties could be felt as an underground
pulsing among some of the leaders on campus. The concerns of our
community often generated from the chapel's basement meeting
rooms. The sanctuary itself, except for early morning services and
choir rehearsal, was often empty and very still. In the evening after
the library closed, I would on occasion stop to sit in the silence.

The big space was made intimate by the surrounding darkness and the candlelight.

One evening, when I was feeling particularly besieged by the concerns churning around and within me, I came to the chapel. It was a wilderness time for me. The way was unclear. I sat in the darkness, focusing on the flame of one of the altar candles. I was alone. The thoughts that came and went have gone now. I do not remember them. What I do remember is the profound sense of stillness that moved from the flame into my being. For what seemed time without end, I felt myself as flame, no separation, only the silent light.

Eventually I regained a sense of myself in the pew looking at the candle on the altar. I do not remember sharing that experience with anyone. The sacred quality of that moment touched into mystery, leading me simply to ponder it in my heart. It is a memory that resides in my soul entire and unfolds on new levels whenever I experience a moment of that kind of stillness and darkness. "A mystery...is something we never finish with. It is never exhausted."

A young mother told me about a moment in which she was caught up in stillness. She had the eyes to see and the space within to simply dwell there. She regularly visited her grandfather in a nursing home. Often she was accompanied by one of her daughters. This day her seven-year-old was sitting on the edge of the bed next to this once gruff and harsh man. He lay there. He could not speak. Slowly he moved his hand toward his great granddaughter, asking for connection without words. She put out her hand in response. For a period of time their hands were entwined as they all sat in silence. The mother was fully present to the sacred mystery of this moment.

Another quality of holy moments is joy. A small group of women were sharing their experiences after hearing the words of May Sarton, "It is essential that true joys be experienced, that the sunrise not leave us unmoved, for civilization depends on true joys.[65] One woman remembered a moment in desert time.

I walk in the desert and it is hot and I am sweating. It all seems so unbearable and then I discover a small flower that has found a place to root and grow. Suddenly it seems like an abundance, an unexpected joy in the barrenness.

"Joy interrupts our absorption," another woman said. "It is a moment of being fully present. I am lost in the moment and not self-conscious." Someone else added: "In that moment, it all seems simple and so easy."

I recall their words now during my writing retreat at Transfiguration Monastery. It is the week before Pentecost. I sit in the chapel after the morning office of Lauds. The chapel is empty. The chapel is full. I am drawn to the great icon of Mary holding the young child Jesus in the center of her lap. It is great in size and in power. Saint Benedict of Nursia and Saint Seraphim of Sarov are included in the small circular icons at the top. They are in attendance, but Mary's presence is palpable to me. Strong body, bold traditional colors, she sits—solid, clear-eyed, and direct in her gaze. Wherever I am in the chapel, her eyes are with me.

I sit now in Mary's presence—the holy feminine strength before me; her gaze engages mine. After a while I close my eyes and let the sun that streams through the large picture window bathe me in its light and warmth. Today at Lauds the words of Saint Basil were read. He spoke of the Holy Spirit being like "the sunshine which permeates all the atmosphere, spreading over land and sea, and yet is enjoyed by each person as though it were for that person alone." I am truly enjoying the sunshine and my sense of the Divine Presence at this moment.

Here I am at the feet of Mary who is wearing bright red shoes—I love that—in the heart of a women's monastery, the chapel, hearing a choir of birdsong carried on the morning air. When I go out I will walk the Great Mother's green shoulders as my feet travel over the verdant spring land. I will gaze at the wooded hills that cup this valley. I am encircled by the Divine Feminine.

Leaving the chapel I follow the dirt road that leads to and from the monastery. The raven who has greeted me at least once a day makes a sweep from its treetop perch near the chapel to the newly cultivated field beside the road. When I first walked here after a night of heavy rain, there were line drawings on the road. Worms were making their way across it by circuitous routes and sometimes even spirals, until a robin or another winged creature discovered and devoured them for breakfast.

As I walk this dry, hard-packed road today, I, too, think of breakfast. I also wonder how a Midwestern Protestant, with paternal family roots sunk in the soil of northern Ireland, came to feel so at home in a Catholic monastery in upstate New York. Perhaps Saint Benedict is smiling now and saying, "It's no surprise. You are only redressing an imbalance in you." And Saint Brigid of Ireland, through whom the Spirit confounded the patriarchy in her day, is probably caught up in delight.[66]

I am learning to trust the power of the Divine working through the communion of saints, past and present, and the community of creatures. I sense our interconnection with "my soul entire" as I stop on the road to watch a goldfinch sing his song; joining Hildegard of Bingen who exclaimed in wonder at creation: "What delight God gives to humankind with all these things."[67]

The little bird puffs out his bright yellow belly and then exhales with his wonderful song. I breathe with him as I watch—amazed by the natural deep breathing of such a tiny creature. Thich Nhat Hanh would smile as I do now, breathing with my brethren.

I notice a less brilliant yellow light in a bush nearby. Bright yellow sings once more; soft yellow responds. Bright yellow flies to a branch beside her. They sing together for a moment and then are off. In a dance of delight, they scallop through the air. Joy!

Reflection

Set time aside to remember holy events and holy moments in your life. Savor one or two. Savoring needs time around it. Give that time to yourself.

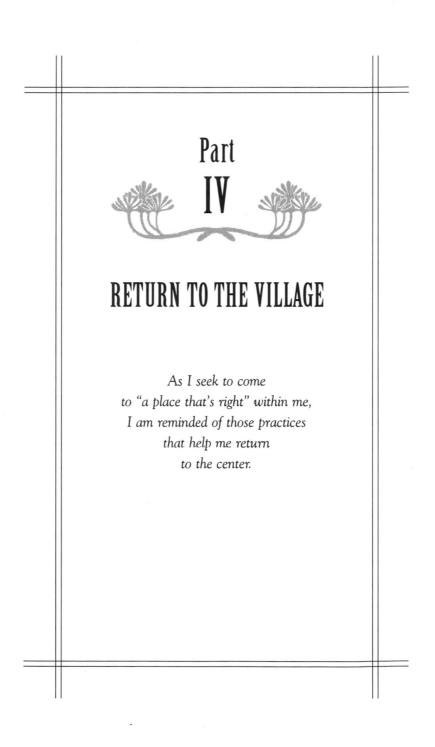

Part
IV

RETURN TO THE VILLAGE

As I seek to come
to "a place that's right" within me,
I am reminded of those practices
that help me return
to the center.

20

CREATING BALANCE IN LIFE

Reflecting on the four life rhythms, I realize that these rhythms weave in and out of my life in many different ways. Each rhythm is essential: the learner, the householder, time in the forest, and then the return to our place of connection: family, work, and community. Together they can create balance for my life.

When we are learners, we give ourselves to one thing alone. Focusing with total attention, we know what it is to be a student. We experience the creative fire of the learner within.

We experience connection, the ground of the householder's life, when we engage in work, family life, and community. It is in this field of relationships that we are most challenged to deepen our spiritual practices.

The necessary condition for time in the forest is time apart from all of these connections. Forest time takes many different forms. It may extend over a long period of outer searching and inner soul work. Or it can be brief moments of solitude in a variety of environments. At some point in all these circumstances, we reach the place of still waters and quiet reflection and our soul is restored.

In the return from time in the forest, we go back to our life in community with a deeper sense of who we are. In my return I come forth with a truer voice, a more authentic way of being in my life as lover, mother, daughter, grandmother, therapist, writer, friend, minister's wife, community member. I return, a sacred work-in-process, to live my way more fully into the compassionate heart of Mystery at work in this world.

I need each of these rhythms for my soul journey. They provide opportunities for focus, connection, solitude, and returning to my daily life in new ways. They seem to be essential for my growth. Like the elements that give life to all creation, they are life-giving rhythms.

21

THE HEADLANDS

It is the morning after Labor Day. I step out into a thick fog as I open the door. The sound of a distant foghorn is muffled by moisture but I hear crickets everywhere. A crow's caw cuts through the mist, while a neighbor comes out of his front door carrying his cat. "Good morning," we say. I pass a policeman checking the parking meters. No one is on the road to the Headlands yet. Mist touches my face as I pass the harbor. Along the way, the deep reds and yellows of garden roses penetrate the gray. Morning glories are open even without the sun. A single gull cries.

As I follow the path to the rock cap, a cat ambles over to meet me. I stroke her as she rubs against me, feeling the morning dew on her coat. The huge rocks that jut out into the ocean are only vague shapes. The breakwater at the mouth of the harbor a few hundred feet to the west is invisible. To the east are sounds of the distant foghorn and buoy bell.

Only days ago the sky was blue and clear. I return in my mind to the "many moods and times of this one good place,"[68] as Thomas Merton said. During a winter nor'easter, the winds here have pushed and buffeted me as I have stood with my back to the land to watch the surf. In the spring the Headlands' vernal pond has contained hundreds of ecstatic frogs in mating time, their sound filling the space. Midsummer the sun scorches the grass on days when sailboats are becalmed near the rocks and the cicadas hum. As autumn progresses, the blueberry bushes make their subtle changes from green to burgundy and then to brittle brown. Finally, the gray hair of winter frost takes over.

My own gray hair is damp now as I sit with the cat beside me, my mind turning over memories of different days. Every day here *is* different. Returning enables me to see, touch, feel, smell that reality once again. Re-turning is a coming back 'round to the familiar through its many forms and expressions.

Turning, itself, is a process. The word comes from the Latin verb *tornare*, which means to turn on a lathe. I have watched a skilled cabinetmaker turn. She marks the center of a piece of wood, which is called a turning, and inserts it into a center point on the lathe that rotates at a high speed. She holds a turning tool against it by placing her hands on the "steady rest." Supporting the tool on the rest, her hand guides the grooves. "It cuts just like butter," she says.

In the nineteenth century, the Shakers recognized this process in their furniture making and in their spiritual practice of dancing. So they sang of "Simple Gifts":

'Tis a gift to be simple, 'tis a gift to be free
'Tis a gift to come down where you ought to be
And when you find yourself in a place that's right
'Twill be in the valley of love and delight.
When true simplicity is gained
To bow and to bend we will not be ashamed
To turn, turn, 'twill be our delight
When in turning, turning we come 'round right.

I re-turn to the Headlands as a spiritual practice to touch the sacred here in the familiar sights, sounds, and creatures. When

I consciously connect with my familiars here in this place, I re-member that the sacred is at the center of all things. As I seek to come to "a place that's right" within me, I am reminded of the importance of those practices that help me return to the center. I am recalled to my own still, center point. With that awareness I can continue to change and be formed by the living of my days.

A slap of wings against the water catches my attention. A bird once resting on the water has now taken off. It is good to rest in this empty space. The fog is quieting. I remember writing in my journal when I was much younger:

Gray days give permission to be.

I catch sight of a small white feather on the rock and pick it up. Holding the feather and looking out to the gray that surrounds me now, I remember a dream of ten years ago. It is still vivid to me.

In my dream I was on the floor of a great Southwestern canyon, with the brilliant blue sky above. High cliffs with caves in them were on all sides. I sensed the presence of wise people in the caves and felt encompassed and blessed by their presence. As I looked up, I saw pristine white feathers against the sky. They were floating down as if sent by the wise ones to me. Seeing a large feather, I ran to it and reached for it. As I took hold, I began to rise with the feather in my hand. Slowly I flew up toward the rim of the canyon.

Since the time of that dream I have been blessed by many people who have shared their wisdom with me. Whenever I find a white feather on my path, I pick it up and think of one of them or a learning—some gift of wisdom that I have received. Today I think of a dear friend whose ashes were scattered off these rocks many years ago. My thoughts move to another friend who died quietly yesterday morning. I offer a prayer of thanksgiving for his wife, who for three years has been with him through all the phases of his cancer, and for his family who surrounded him in these last days.

I retrace my steps down the road toward home. A friend comes to her door. We greet each other and I continue on, thinking of the way she has created a new life for herself since her husband's death. Around the corner, tall cosmos catches my eye. A deep pink blossom is bowing and bending on its stem, reminding me of the woman who tends this garden. Right now she is on her way into Boston by train. The daily commute has become a form of time apart for her. She calls it forest time.

As I return from my time of solitude, I give thanks for all the people in the village who have touched my life with their wisdom. I rejoice in the cosmos, which reminds me "to bow and to bend." The words of "Simple Gifts" sing inside me. They recall me to turn, turn around the center that is my true being and the place of my union with God, so that I, too, can "come 'round right." And when I am there, in that inner space that's right, I sense that I am home, home "in the valley of love and delight."

Reflection: A Journal Exercise

Objective: To deepen self-awareness.

Time for exercise: Thirty minutes.

Materials needed: Colored pens/pencils.

Procedure:

1. Spend time with the words of "Simple Gifts."*

    > 'Tis a gift to be simple, 'tis a gift to be free
    > 'Tis a gift to come down where you ought to be
    > And when you find yourself in a place that's right
    > 'Twill be in the valley of love and delight.
    > When true simplicity is gained
    > To bow and to bend we will not be ashamed
    > To turn, turn, 'twill be our delight
    > When in turning, turning we come 'round right.

2. First copy the words into your journal slowly, with care as a monk might have copied a sacred manuscript. Then sit with the words.

3. Using your nondominant hand and/or your colored pens or pencils, circle words that attract your attention. Choose colors that match the energy that you feel toward that word.

4. When you have responded by circling those words, go to a new page. Place your chosen words on the new page. Play with the words in relation to one another until you have a sense of completion.

5. Take time to see what you have created. Then live with it and let the words inform you in your daily life.

---

*If the words of this Shaker hymn do not speak to you, choose a poem, a psalm, lyrics, or a short piece of writing that is meaningful to you at this time in your life. Then follow the instructions for this exercise.

THE CONTEMPLATIVE WITHIN

"How has your time away changed your life?" asked a woman who is an artist and lives alone. She was one of a group of women who invited me to speak to them about our sabbatical journey. Their invitation offered the needed spark of energy to further integrate that experience. It had been almost a year since our return from those weeks of participating in the life of three contemplative communities.

I chose to call the talk: "My Journey with Mary and Martha."

The preparation for it offered an opportunity to reflect right in the middle of my life in the village. I began by remembering the last days before we left on our sabbatical. I felt spent and without the reserves that I needed to reach out to others. In my heart, there was no space left for hospitality. The feelings that I had were focused into one: longing. I was longing for a more contemplative way of living. When Gregory the Great summarized the Christian contemplative tradition, he used the phrase "resting in God."[69] I longed to be in a place where I felt permission to let myself rest in God.

I remembered the origin of the word "contemplative." It comes from two Latin words, *con* and *templus*: *con* means with; *templus*, holy or sacred space. At its root, contemplative means being with sacred space. It is natural to associate temples with the sacred.

They were often built to mark the place of sacred happenings, constructed after an experience of the holy occurred. Something in all of us wants to mark moments of the inbreaking of the Divine into our lives.

I recall the account of the three disciples who experienced the transfigured presence of Jesus accompanied by Moses and Elijah. Immediately after that holy encounter, they wanted to build booths on Mount Tabor to honor and mark that place which had become sacred (Matt. 17:1–8). The space was made sacred first by what occurred before, within, and among those disciples. Their openness and availability enabled them to be present to that holy moment of transfiguration. Then came the desire to create a structure to claim that space as holy ground.

Originally the events themselves are sacred space. Then come the structures, temples, shrines, and churches that mark in time and place what was experienced as timeless and beyond place. We return to those sacred places with a longing to touch the reality behind those moments once again. For in the holy moment is the sense of coming home, being where we are meant to be.

The contemplative within each one of us longs to return home to "the sacred space deep within me," as one woman calls it. "It is in that soul space where I sense my unique connection with the deepest part of myself and how I am connected to God and other people." A gifted musician and mother of a teenager, she acknowledges and touches a common longing in many of us for an awakened sense of our connection with the source of our being, which is eternal.

"Homing" is a word used by Clarissa Pinkola Estés in her work with women. "Within the soul is the homing device. We can all find our way back."[70] Our paths for returning and our experience of home may be different. However, we have in common the longing of our souls to return to the source of true being and to live out of that place more fully. It is the contemplative within each of us who recognizes this place of home and knows how to dwell there.

For many years I felt that this longing part of me was in conflict with the active/doer part. When I was a young mother, the thin line between the extrovert and introvert in me was often a place of struggle. In my religious tradition of biblical stories, the account of Jesus' visit with the sisters, Martha and Mary, Luke 10:38–42, seemed to represent my inner conflict.

Martha was in the kitchen, "worried and distracted over many things" as she tried to prepare another meal for Jesus who was often a guest in their home. Meanwhile, Mary peacefully sat in the presence of Jesus listening to his every word. When Martha called out to Jesus: "Don't you care that my sister has left me to do all the work by myself? Tell her to help me." Jesus' response seemed to affirm Mary.

> Martha, Martha. You are worried and distracted about many things; there is need of only one thing. Mary has chosen the better part, which shall not be taken from her. (Luke 10: 41–42)

I identified with Martha. Mary's role in that situation was not likely to be mine, not in the drama of my life. There was little time to sit and be still. Jesus' words did, however, seem to speak to my longing to be focused and concentrated. Over the years I have returned to this story, as do many women, because I have been drawn to it, angered by it, and frustrated because it seemed to present an either/or situation which I could not accept. Without knowing it I was following the contemplative practice of living with a passage of scripture. Among Benedictines the practice of prayerful reading of scripture and other "spiritual writings" is called *lectio divina*. It has been referred to as a form of "rumination."[71] Different from reflection and scholarly work, it is a way of "chewing on" an idea until you can digest it and some of its substance becomes part of you.

Lectio is also a way to go deep in the familiar over time. After years of living with this story, I discovered a way beneath my impasse with Mary and Martha. I returned to the words attributed to Jesus, who clearly loved both women (John 11:5). Now I hear the words differently. I hear the emphasis on Mary's choice, not on Mary's nature.

The one thing needed was to be fully present to what was before each of them. For Martha, it was the activity of serving, providing hospitality. For Mary, it was making hospitable space within to listen to the rabbi. The choice to be with this task, this person, this object as sacred, means to be present with the fullness of our self—that choice is "the better part."

The activist, doer, server may be predominant in some of us, perhaps 70 to 80 percent of the time. There are those who may be 10 percent doer and 90 percent listener. Others may have a 50–50 proportion of the activist and the receptive listener. And it is just as possible for me to be "worried and distracted" while sitting in meditation or listening to a loved one as it is when I am preparing a meal for guests. The challenge in this story is to choose to be fully present whether I am actively serving or quietly sitting.

Through living my way into the story of Mary and Martha, I discovered that within each of us there is a contemplative dimension that is deeper than that of the doer or the listener. That core part of us, the contemplative within, dwells in that deepest dimension beneath all polarities. From that place of soul home we can make our choices as to how we live out our particular expression of self. The contemplative within each of us does not challenge us to change our nature, but to consciously choose to be with our commitments. In doing so, we can recognize the events and people in our lives and our inner journeys as sacred.

My Quaker friend, who had to learn not to overextend herself because of her illness, became my teacher by her example. "We think where it's at is out there," she said. "Maybe it is right where we are." At Pendle Hill, the Quaker Center for Study and Contemplation, all students and sojourners have a job. Her work assignment was to tend the candles in the dining room, trimming wicks, removing stubs, and replacing those that were burned down. "Doing it with love is what makes it sacred," she said.

As I work in my own kitchen now I remember my particular job of washing vegetables for the large gathering at Pendle Hill. Following my friend's example, I consciously chose to be single-minded: one task at a time. Gunilla Norris speaks beautifully of this practice in her book *Being Home*. She asks, "How then do we come home and spiritually dwell there? In my own life I have found no better way than to value and savor the sacredness of daily living, to rely on repetition, that humdrum rhythm which heals and steadies."[72] And so with gratitude for teachers along the way, I now practice choosing to notice color, shape, texture as I dip each vegetable in cold, clear water. I go at my own pace. Peel the carrot, dice the peppers, wash the lettuce, slice the onion. It is the conscious choosing to be present that truly is "the better part."

These thoughts and memories wove together in my talk to the women that day several years ago. I felt very centered as I spoke. I responded to the question, "How has this time apart changed your life?" by speaking of the commitment that I made at

Transfiguration Monastery to follow some daily practices as a way to deepen my union with God. I came away from their meeting grateful for the opportunity to put words to my experience.

The next day my husband left for a few days. I had errands to do, places to go, clients to see. I needed to eat lunch before the next client. I also needed to go to the bank before it closed. I put rice on the stove and hurried to the bank. Then I remembered a book that I wanted to give to someone that afternoon, so I went to the bookstore. Starting to browse there, I suddenly remembered the rice. I ran the three blocks home to hear the smoke alarm wailing inside the house as I turned the corner.

The house was filled with smoke. My lunch of brown rice had burned into a huge black rice cake. Dense smoke rolled through the downstairs and quickly traveled to the upstairs bedrooms. I silenced the alarm by opening doors and windows. The thick smoke began to move out, but the acrid smell remained. I did not sleep well that night. The smell kept reminding me of how easily I had become distracted about many things. How quickly I forgot to be mindful.

Two days earlier I had felt so centered as I spoke with the women about the contemplative within. However, the black rice cake and the lingering smell of smoke reminded me that I am a learner. There are second chances and I can return to my practice of being with what is before me. I can re-choose to be present to one task at a time. Grace does provide the opportunity to return— to begin again. The village is a place where I can start over. It is where the adult learner dwells.

The learner is always a beginner. In play, the child can always begin again. As an adult the ability to laugh and to play provides balance for me when I get too serious about my intentions. As I reflect on the total experience of connecting with the story of

Mary and Martha and of my burning the rice, I recall the words of Thomas Merton which I keep on my bulletin board.

Merton's village was a Trappist monastery. Most of his work was done in his hermitage. Yet he influenced people all around the globe. Through his writing, social activists, world leaders, and solitary monks learned to trust the contemplative within.

> We live in the fullness of time.
> Every moment is God's own good time, his *kairos*
> The whole thing boils down to giving ourselves in prayer a
>   chance to realize that we have what we seek.
> We don't have to rush after it.
> It is there all the time,
> and if we give it time it will make itself known to us.[73]

In the literal boiling down of my experience, I was reminded once again that daily practice, moment by moment, is the way of the learner in the midst of the fullness of time. And if I do not rush after what I seek, it will indeed make itself known to me, one way or another.

Reflection

1. What opportunity for learning seems to be wanting your attention right now?

2. In what ways do you feel like a beginner in regard to that learning?

3. Can you recognize and celebrate the learner in you as you respond to this opportunity?

23

ANGELS WITH BOOTS ON

This morning I am conscious of my well-worn hiking boots as I climb over the rocks on the Headlands. Instead of my usual path, I choose to go close to the water's edge. This way takes me to a sitting rock from which I can view the sunrise. Just in time, I watch the sun's rays make their way behind and through the clouds on the eastern horizon. Shades of scarlet to pink begin to spread, backlighting an extraordinary cloud form. A soft, feathered great left wing and then the dancing flame of a right wing emerges. Angel wings unfolding before my eyes. Oh, how wonderful... soft, alive, proclaiming, announcing, celebrating: healing for this weary world. I sit, not moving, for the display of color lasts only minutes.

Grateful for the support of my boots, I climb back up the rocks. A phrase comes to me: angels with boots on. That's what it takes to walk the walk of this life. I picture an angel, not a Christmas ornament angel, but a being full of light and life, soft and embracing, strong as a dancing flame. She stands in her fullness in the middle of a muddy, stony field with sturdy boots on her feet. Grounded, in touch with earthy realities, she is also aware of the flame of her true being and the source of that holy fire.

It is time to return home. I hold the image and think about the many women, angels for me, who are involved in their daily

lives in this honest, open way. They express stability by being
fully present to what is before them, and yet they are available
and open to the Holy One moving through them, each in her
own unique way. They live out what I now understand to be
hospitality, or what Gabriel Marcel described as "availability" or
"human openness."

> To be available is to be so uncluttered by a sense of one's own
> importance, so unthreatened by the strangeness of others,
> that one may enter immediately into communion.[74]

I am blessed to be in communion with women who live their lives
with this kind of openness. They have been and are my mentors
and my teachers.

One is the single mother of a teenaged daughter and older
sons, who as a child felt her own "disabilities" and differences
as a learner. Now an artist, she struggles to support her family
while discovering her ability as a teacher. She draws on her direct
experience of the holy in nature and shares it with children. In
her classes she helps them to celebrate their unique abilities and
their differences.

It is this real, down-to-earth openness to the Spirit that lies at
the heart of hospitality: that core commitment of the Benedictine
community. It was my intention as our sabbatical time unfolded
to *learn* more *about* hospitality, which can be defined as kind and
generous reception of the one who comes as guest. Instead, I
experienced hospitable space developing within as a guest in the
three communities we visited. I discovered that when mental,
emotional, and spiritual space is cluttered within me, I am not
available for the task at hand. The one thing needed for both
generous hospitality and receptive inner space is a practice that is
kind to and nourishes the contemplative within.

Benedict of Nursia was wise in his counsel about hospitality. Even though he encouraged community members to "receive everyone as Christ," he also offered very practical advice so that the contemplative nature of their communal life would not be disrupted. It was important to find a balanced way to offer what they uniquely had to give: hospitable space for guests, especially the poor, the stranger, and the pilgrim.[75] Benedict knew that the community needed to provide enough help to those in charge of receiving guests so that they did not feel burdened and were able to welcome all guests as Christ.

We need to be wise with ourselves, to recognize that we have limits to our reserves and our capacity to devote attention to others as sacred mysteries. Present circumstances and our own personal makeup are important factors. There are times when our well is dry. It is necessary to recognize the signals for this condition. For example, when my reserves are low, I often push myself harder than ever and take on more. I get super-responsible and then overburdened. These familiar reactions are signals to me to return to practices that restore my soul.

At times like this, it is helpful to clarify what we *are* able to do. For instance, when someone calls on us to be there for them, we might respond in new ways. "I would like to be really present to you and I can listen for ten minutes." Or "I will call you back in the morning when I can be more present." For the parent who is being petitioned by a young child, the response can be as simple as this: "I have to go to the bathroom. I'll be out in a few minutes." For an older child we can model the need for time apart. "I need to be alone right now. In a little while I will be more able to think about it with you." By stating what is true for us in that moment, we honor the integrity of the other person as well as ourselves. This, too, is a form of hospitality.

Although my angels with boots on are very different in their life styles, they are similar in their sacred intent. I will never forget my first view of Sister Donald Corcoran, prioress of Transfiguration Monastery. She was dressed in the long-skirted, Benedictine working habit and her work boots as she strode down the dirt road to mount the cab of the community pickup truck. It is she who names the intent of "receptivity of heart" as the essence of the contemplative way. This orientation, she clarifies, does not foster the extraordinary mystical experience, but it does foster every-day openness and "the listening heart."[76] When we practice this kind of deep listening, we offer hospitable space, and the other discovers what is within him or her.

Another community, kindred in spirit to the Benedictines, continues also to teach me about "receptivity of heart" and hospitable space. Like Transfiguration Monastery, it too came into being because of a shared vision. Fifteen years ago a small group of women and one man, laypeople and nuns, went through a period of forest time together. It was a time of discerning the form for a vision that they held, "a vision of hospitality." Rosemary Haughton was part of that group who, when they "saw and loved an old house in Gloucester . . . knew it was the right place to realize the vision that we shared." They left familiar forms of house-holding, jobs, and family to begin this venture called Wellspring House.[77]

Hospitality isn't just about having friends to dinner, it is about breaking barriers, about sharing, about openness to newness. Being hospitable is about opening a home to others and also about making homes possible. It means welcoming strangers and discovering friends.[78]

Nancy Schwoyer, now executive director of Wellspring House, reflects on her choice to leave her religious order "and to live out of the tradition of hospitality and welcoming."

We have shared our home with three hundred families and helped them to find permanent homes. It is so fundamental. That is where my grounding is. Home making is the heart of the shelter. As a feminist I have come to feel homemaking is a real paradigm for our work at Wellspring on almost every level. Making a home together is so central to my life. It is a way of saying that the hierarchy of tasks doesn't work. All need to participate in making an environment that is welcoming.

In my years in the convent great emphasis was placed on taking care of things. That came out of our vow of poverty and I don't think I appreciated it until the experience of Wellspring. I got trained in caring and hospitality. Now I have come to understand how very spiritual that is. It affects the choices that we make.

For instance, we grow our large flower and vegetable garden organically and we compost. I think about getting in touch with the earth as home while I carry the compost out, a very ordinary task, but it is not ordinary. The waste that I carry will become that which nourishes next year's vegetables or flowers. I am mindful of this: returning things to the earth and knowing that the earth is going to return something back to us.

As a people we have lost our sense of connection with earth as home. We have distanced ourselves so much from growing things and from the practical things that go into making a home. For me part of the human task is to make this earth a home, to make our communities a home, to provide spaces and places where people can be at home. We need to intentionally make hospitable space available for people.

Wellspring has a new educational wing and expanded pro- grams. Yet they continue to keep the shelter at the heart of this home. When asked why they have been successful in this work, Nancy says,

It is because we have kept the reality of homelessness present. Keeping the mission and the human need literally at the center of the house has made a real difference.

To share their home with homeless families and many vol- unteers draws on the resources of the core community. Nancy speaks of the familiar practices to which she returns for her replenishment. These rituals of returning are essential to her.

Going deeper in the familiar of our householding life here depends on a commitment to things in my life on a regular basis: our prayer before dinner, the shelter staff coming to- gether for prayer at the beginning of the new week, our Sunday morning ritual. We have discovered that in do- ing things intentionally week after week, day after day, something sacred breaks through. We have come to know and recognize that taking time for prayer and reflection is essential, if we want to be a hospitable space.

SOME OF US ACTUALLY DO END the householding years as we have known them and choose to go into the forest for a period of time in order to discern how to be in our life with others in a new way. A woman in her sixties made a radical change for this purpose.

I knew for seven years that when my son Don's inevitable death from AIDS occurred, I must move from my homophobic community and begin a new life elsewhere. He knew that, too. He encouraged me to begin the process before he died. So I did. During his last years I retired from teaching high school. At sixty-three, I put my affairs in order, chose a retirement location, and prepared to move.

Immediately after his death I sold my home, found a new community in the East, and then physically moved. I said goodbye to all I had loved for most of my life: my home, my friends, work, landscape, and my history. But the things I left in the ground—rosebushes, flowering crabs planted each Mother's Day, and the graves of my two sons were the hardest to leave.

In mid-December, I uprooted myself and moved to a beautiful but alien coastal New England town. I rented a little house in the forest near the sea. The only person I knew was the real estate woman who helped me find a home. "I hope you don't feel too isolated here," she warned. At that point, isolation appealed to me. I left the chaos and danger of the urban school where I was teaching, the constant ringing of the telephone, and the noise of the freeway a few blocks away.

Now the pounding of the surf against the rocks woke me at night. The dark was darker and blacker, but the stars were brighter and closer. At sunrise of the second day, I saw two eagles swoop over the water as they fished. But the phone never rang, few cars passed on the road, and I was not ready to venture into the village several miles away. Indeed I was isolated: alone in the forest, alone with my grief, and alone with my God in the silence.

I listened. I wrote. I read. I cried. I slept. For the first time in fifty busy, busy years, I had to face myself. How had it happened that I had lost so many: parents, aunts and uncles, a brother, a husband, and two sons? Why was I alive, a woman who had been near death twice in the recent past. . . . A woman who gladly would have given her own life for first one son, then another? I was no longer a daughter, a niece, a wife, nor the mother of two. Who was I now? I had been a teacher; what was I now? I was a loving friend and neighbor, but who were my friends and neighbors now? I was filled with self-doubt and self-pity. Had I done the right thing or was it another bad decision? What was I supposed to *do*?

I was alone. And it was good—the silence, the loneliness, and finally the freedom. I walked and walked for miles each day, no matter what the weather. I prayed as I walked, immersed in nature until I too became part of creation. I became a child again, a child of the Holy Spirit who had led me to this place of rest and renewal.

I prayed throughout the day for Don and those I had lost, but after awhile I began praying for those I had loved and "kept." The circle of prayer widened and I began praying for those who lived in fear of violence, abuse, of war and disease, especially AIDS. I prayed for caregivers and others who mourned. I prayed for the whole world.

By mid-February I knew I had survived. I wanted to live. I didn't know why, but I knew God's purpose would unfold. I knew it was time: I needed people and laughter and touch. I went to church in the village finally, my first encounter with the stern, reserved New Englanders I feared. They seemed warm and welcoming, but I was careful. I wore dark clothes, kept quiet, and rejoiced in receiving the eucharist again. Fortunately, they were friendlier than I!

This woman's circle of caring expanded in her new village. She eventually became a lay eucharistic minister, a speaker at schools and colleges about homophobia, and a member of a laywomen's order. She returned to school to expand her skills and now teaches by coaching others in their writing. Old friends from a distance and new friends gather in her home. "I am full of thanksgiving," she says on her seventieth birthday. "I have walked in the valley of the shadow of death and have emerged into the light."

As I walk home from the Headlands, I think of other women who have shared their stories as they walk their particular roads. There were the parents of preschoolers with special needs who supported one another in a group that I was privileged to lead. I was deeply touched by the quiet heroism of those young women and their husbands.

A friend who was in the initial stages of Lou Gehrig's disease spoke to me of her joy in creating. Truly an angel with boots on, she cherished her gift of self-expression, savoring each day with heightened awareness.

Using the power of creativity to make beautiful things makes me feel connected to myself more than any other activity that I do. I love the sensation of my mind and my hands working—of being pleasurably absorbed in the task.

A young mother expressed her longing for time to explore "within myself the different things that have interested me. I have always wanted to find the more artistic side of myself. I would like to explore that at some point." She is realistic about her situation.

Right now my working full time is what I have to do for our family but I don't want to miss watching my son grow. So far I have been fortunate because I have been there during the big moments like when he rolled over or pulled up or crawled. I have been able to be there.

Being there, being fully present when she is there, is this young woman's practice. She is an angel with boots on. Her feet are firmly planted in the reality of her days. She owns her longings and, at the same time, opens herself and is available to the sacred in the present moment. She, too, has been my teacher.

These angels are still with me when I return home from my walk to find an urgent message from a single mother in our church. She has to go to the hospital immediately. "Who can take care of my children now and be with them tonight?"

Thoughts go through my head.

> I've got to do it. How can I do it?
> A group is coming in an hour for a quiet day.
> What shall I do?
> How do I balance these two calls for hospitality?

Words come from within.

> Ask for help—turn to your community.
> Be present now.
> Keep your boots on.
> This is an opportunity to draw on your practice.

As I pick up the phone, I call on the strength of Mary, the clarity of Mary, the willingness of Mary to help me discern what to do: one step at a time.

"I want to help and I will get help," I say into the phone. "Can you wait a few minutes? I will call you back."

The place for my practice *is* right where I am standing. Here. Now. I am glad that I still have my boots on.

Reflection: A Journal Exercise

Objective: To identify what may be emerging.

Time: Twenty minutes.

Materials needed: Journal, pen or pencil.

Procedure: Respond to the questions in the order suggested.

A group of women were discussing this chapter. One member was wrestling with the conflict between self-care and "being Christ-like, unselfish, ready to play the servant, caring, and going the extra mile."

Her questions to others were: "How do we prospective angels find the balance? How can we know and then declare our limits to those in need? And most importantly, how can we develop discernment for situations that will ultimately prove self-destructive?"

As a way to address her questions, experiment with the following suggestions.

1. Make a list of women you know whom you might call "angels with boots on," women who are honest about their circumstances, very real in their struggles and frustrations, yet have a spaciousness within—they offer hospitable space.

2. What are the qualities that you admire in them? List the qualities beside their names. Note how the different qualities that you focus on help to create balance for these people.

3. As you reflect on these qualities, consider this: often the qualities that we notice in others are the very qualities that are emerging in ourselves.

24

THE DOULA

The phone rings. It is our youngest daughter.

"Mom, I want you to be my doula," she says.

"A doula?" I ask.

"It means a woman who has experienced childbirth who can be supportive to the mother who is giving birth. It really means being a presence."

I heard her words "supportive" and "presence" and from somewhere within me I heard my words: "Yes. I can do that. I am deeply touched." It was as if a part of me knew that I could learn from this task, knew that it was an opportunity to be with the sacred. However, for one who feels most productive when I have an agenda, to be asked to be simply a presence was initially frightening, although ultimately freeing.

"What will I *do*? I don't know all the things you know about birth now. When I had my babies, I didn't have my glasses on to see what was going on in the mirror." My most recent experience was as an observer at our first grandson's birth. My job was to take pictures. My mind raced to create a plan once more. I need a class, a book. I need to be prepared!

She said it once again. "Be with me. We have taken the classes; the nurse and doctor will do their jobs. I need you simply to be present."

What a request! She really wants me to be with her as she labors through this work of bringing forth life. What a privilege. I began to feel excitement. Later I spent a session with an experienced midwife who spoke of the value of a presence. She showed me a video of a birth that confirmed what I had learned from watching my oldest daughter and son-in-law bring their son into the world. I felt encouraged for my new role.[79]

I didn't realize that being with my daughter as a doula would also include a ten-day waiting period. Her baby had an agenda of her own. I wrote in my journal on the ninth day:

> This *is* waiting. I feel Mary's presence in this waiting and not knowing. For me it is a real exercise in being here, now—just as I am in this day. Being around to encourage has been a practice in doula support. I hope I can do it when it gets labor-intensive. I seem to be able to go with the Spirit and be in the stream, like swimming with the current, stroking, moving, playing in the waters as they course on their way. I remember saying many years ago: "Oh God, you are to me a River." I am in you now.

On Mother's Day I took the opportunity to reflect on what was involved in a doula's job.

> I am being asked to listen, empathize, support, encourage, hold in my prayers—to be a spiritual/emotional doula. That is my role here now.
>
> They say that the doula's presence makes the birth less intense, less difficult, shortens the labor, and enables the mother to cooperate with the natural process.
>
> Perhaps this is also the way to be with adult children as they grow.

And then the day arrived—night actually—when all else faded into the background as the movement began within my daughter. The momentum toward birth took over and became the focus of all our energy for the next eighteen hours.

> Being with each moment. I had a sense of being in the flow. Only this: to be present and responsive, without forethought. I felt a knowing of how to be in that moment coming from within me, below my head, a surrender to the knowing— fluid, like the Tao, the Spirit, the river of God's creative energy. The image of water kept coming, water finding its way around stone, keeps on moving.... Being one with the moving waters.

At the same time I felt focused, alert, and awake, ready to respond and ready to wait: a drink, a towel, a word of encouragement, silence, an arm. I took my cues from my laboring daughter who, with her husband at her side, was rocking, breathing, walking, bathing, squatting, breathing, reaching heights of pain then breathing, resting in between throughout the laboring hours to that moment of the final push. And then . . . such joy!

Within this birthing experience, there was a birth of knowing in me. It was a body/soul kind of knowing that drew on the reservoir of the contemplative within me. My experience of being a doula for my daughter brought together all the rhythms of my life as a woman. Perhaps that is the nature of holy events.

The time surrounding my granddaughter's birth was an intimate family time, different from the ongoing aspects of my regular householding life. It also had elements of time in the forest, with moments to reflect on my experience. In addition it was an opportunity for learning with "my soul entire." It drew on all that I am, enabling me to learn more about trust. After this experience

I returned to the village, my home, work, and community, with a deeper awareness of the resources available within me.

My role was so clear: to be a support to her. The focus was single, just like the one-ing of the push. Only one job: to be with the sacred moment—now.

Things worked, came into being, got resolved not by my anticipated plan but by my being aware, alert, taking cues from what is before me, and working together with the ones laboring to bring forth new life.

This learning transferred to my work. The way of the doula describes my process as a counselor working with people who choose to do soul work. A woman's choice to go deeper into a blocked or hard place is creative work. It involves preparation, gestation, and laboring in order to bring forth new life when it is ready to come. It is a privilege to be a supportive presence, engaged with another in this process.

The experience with my daughter was a gift. It expanded my understanding of hospitality by providing an opportunity for what Sister Donald described as soulful living. "To grow as a soulful person means to grow in human heartedness, in depth and interiority and in greater and greater capacity for the Spirit."[80] That inner space was opened up within me.

Some people seem to know how to provide hospitable space naturally and with ease. Others learn this as one of the rich fruits of a life's harvest. And most of us need spiritual practices that develop this quality so that we can respond when we are called to be a doula. I find that the simple practice of repeating a psalm while I am walking, doing dishes, or swimming supports my intention to become open and available. I fit the phrases with my breathing.

Create in me a clean [or clear] heart, O God...
and sustain in me a willing spirit. (Psalm 51:10, 12)

The call comes in different forms. For many years a group of people gathered weekly in our living room to offer support to each other in our personal and spiritual journeys. Sometimes we offered tough love and sometimes we listened. Now one member is dying of Lou Gehrig's disease. Other group members spend time with her during the week, privileged to share in the sacredness of who she is at this time in her living and her dying. We are present with her while this courageous woman shares the depth of her soul work. One day she types on her assistive device: "I have touched the place I always wanted to go but never seemed to get there before."

Another community of people became doulas and their experience was described by Rosemary Houghton, associate director of Wellspring House.

Two guests came to our home on Easter weekend—one was a young woman and the other was the one Saint Francis called Sister Death.... This was a young woman who only a few years ago had been a guest at the Wellspring family shelter with her little boy. They moved into a home of their own—and then she became ill with cancer. After surgery, and many treatments, she finally knew that her fight for life was almost over, but there was no family member to whom she could go.... We asked her if she would like to come home to Wellspring and she said yes.

With the help of Hospice of the North Shore, a nurse, and a social worker from the local hospital, this community kept vigil.

So we celebrated Easter. On Saturday evening, while our friend lay in one room, in another we lighted the Easter candle and sang songs of new life. Through the evening we visited her, tended her, and one of us slept in the next room to be available in the night.

On Easter Day, friends came for dinner, among them the nine-year-old boy whose mother was dying. He shared in the celebration, played with other children in the sunny yard, then came to say goodbye. People moved from the festival meal to the place of waiting; the room was a holy place, with flowers and prayers and candles and music and loving words and touches, another Easter banquet.

That evening Sister Death came gently and quietly. Afterward, for a long time, people continued to come and go, to sit in silence or to share memories, then to help clear up the Easter meal, then spend a little more time with the living and the dead.[81]

For centuries women have been doulas at the time of death, being a presence in different ways. A woman tending her father in the last hours of his life climbs into the bed to hold him while he lets go into death. Two sisters keep vigil in the early hours of the morning with their mother who is a soprano soloist but can no longer respond. They quietly sing hymns and favorite songs together. One daughter reads aloud the scripture that will be read at her mother's funeral service, knowing that the sense of hearing remains longer than all other senses. As the sun rises they move her bed to the window so that she can feel the light of dawn as she quietly slips into the Light.

A sister chooses to be a doula for her own sister. She recalls the fourteen-month period from the diagnosis of Karen's ovarian cancer until her death. After nine months of chemotherapy and a second surgery, the cancer was still noted in multiple sites in her abdomen and the doctors gave her no hope of survival.

Karen and I shared so much during our lives as sisters that it was only a natural extension that we should share her death. I knew with absolute clarity that I could not wait to spend time with her. When I quit my job it wasn't to take care of Karen—it was to *be* with her. She decided not to try radiation but chose some "alternative treatments." We went together to a health institute and I followed the regimen of wheat grass juice and living foods along with her. She continued to be hopeful and believe in a miracle.

During the holiday months we spent our time together. By February she was hospitalized, attending my son's wedding on a day-pass. Discharged a week later she was soon readmitted to the hospital, never to go home again. I spent the days there with her. We talked about a variety of things—some serious, some silly. I did all the little things she could no longer do for herself. Later we talked about how helpless she felt when she couldn't reach anything beyond arm's length and how helpless I felt because I couldn't "fix" things for her.

Miracles did occur—but not the one that brought the cure. Together we counted our blessings, which included each other. Another was this: when the time came, she was ready to die and I was able to let her go. I remember this journey with Karen as one that profoundly impacted my life.

My sister overwhelmed me with her capacity for forgiveness towards a nurse who made an error which necessitated another surgery. She taught me by example. She was rich in faith, humor, hope, kindness, and love. I can't help but think

of the "Magic Penny" song which says: "Love is something
when you give it away, you end up having more."

Women tend women in different kinds of situations. A friend
of many years called me long distance. Her daughter was getting
married. "Will you be my doula during the wedding?" She was
asking me to simply be a presence with her, taking my cues from
her as she carried out her tasks. How many others have done this
at weddings, births, funerals, and other life events in the village.
The call to be a doula may come to us in ways that are not
always direct. Our spiritual practices help us to maintain open
space within, so that we can be awake and alert in our response.
To be a doula offers a form of hospitality that is a gift sorely needed
in our global village.

As caregivers and householders it is also important to ask for
doulas to be with us in the living of our days. We need to practice
being direct in asking for this support. We may simply need to say:
"Will you listen to me? I don't need you to solve anything—just
be present to me—receive me." Stating our need for a doula is
one way of honoring the sacred mystery that we are.

We also need to encourage each other to become doulas for
ourselves, to use those very skills to tend the life within us. This
can be a creative process, a healing process, a birthing process.
We must set time apart from our other duties for our inner labor.
We need to listen for cues, allow the time that it needs, and
provide hospitable space so that new life can come forth within
us. One fifty-year-old woman said, "We are learning to give birth
to ourselves."

As with pregnancy, when women make the passage through
menopause our bodies often get our attention. At this time we
can choose to be really present and cooperate with the body/

soul changes that take place. We can be a doula for ourselves by taking cues from our body, working with it, learning from it, and honoring the process and the labor that brings us to newness in our life as women.

The life passage of menopause offers us another opportunity to go deep in the familiar, the familiar of our body. It also provides good preparation in learning how to be managers of our own health care, a skill much needed as we grow into our elder years. The word manage comes from *manus*, which is the Latin word for hand. When we take our health care into our own hands, it is like riding a horse. We hold the reins in our hands firmly but not grasping, so that we can work with the energy and spirit of the horse. Our intention is to develop companionship with the horse. We need to work like a doula with our bodies in this same way, cooperatively rather than forcefully imposing our will and control.

As I continue my pilgrimage through my sixth decade and into my elder years, I like to hold the image of myself traveling as a doula on horseback.

Reflection

1. When have you been called upon to be with someone simply as a presence?

2. When have you needed someone to be that for you?

3. In what ways are you learning how to be a doula for yourself?

25

GRATITUDE

Once again I am longing to rest in God.

A friend says, "Come to my house. It is quiet. I will leave you alone. There is a room and a bed and no one can reach you. The space can be yours for twenty-four hours."

I know it is what I need. "Yes," I say. "Yes."

It is afternoon as I enter the room that is to be mine. Quiet colors of grey-blue and white surround me. Touches of beauty are everywhere. Bright red tomatoes fill an earthen bowl. How tired I feel. I need time away from people and yet I feel grateful for the richness of those who are in my life.

As a way to make a transition to a time of retreat, I sit by a window with my journal and list all the people and my feelings about them. I recall the saying that gratitude and anxiety cannot occupy the same space. Here in this place I am emptying out with gratitude. My thoughts move from family members to friends to church and community and then to the beauty outside the window: bare trees, evergreens, and the winter birds in the high bushes nearby. I spill out my thoughts onto paper and then finally write:

> It is so quiet here. I need rest.
> I am so grateful for a place to rest.

I am hungry. In the kitchen I find a note with simple instructions, which also tell me what is available to eat. Bread, made by a mutual friend, and tea, which will be soothing for my stomach that has been churning in the past weeks. The hot tea steams in the stone mug with its cobalt blue band. I bite into toasted bread. As I chew its goodness slowly, I also enjoy the taste of friendship: women tending women.

Along with my journal and my overnight bag, I have brought a vigil light and an icon. I chose to bring an icon of the face of Christ. This one is usually the focus for our meditation area at home. The steady gaze of Christ in this particular icon is compassionate and strong. I have need for this doorway into his presence during these hours apart.

Darkness comes early in the winter. As I sit before the icon, I cannot impose artificial light. The vigil light is enough. I gaze at the face with the stillness of night surrounding me. My mind continues to go from here to there, thought to thought. I hear from somewhere deep within: "Be with me for a while," gentle yet commanding. In the quiet of this place it is all that I want to do.

"Be with me for a while." These words now take over. "Be present to me, open yourself to me for a while." My aching shoulders release. My stomach unclutches. I let my face relax. A dialogue begins within me and I write it out in my journal.

JOAN: In your presence I want to move slowly. I want to breathe deeply. I want to simply be.

JESUS: Be with me for a while—not just a moment—for a while. Leave behind your agenda. Tomorrow is soon enough for that. Be with me—right now.

JOAN: As I gaze at your face in the flickering candlelight, for a time the flame stands still and you, it, and I are

encircled—quiet—still. I do not want to leave you or
the quiet of the night.

JESUS: Go in peace. I am always with you.

JOAN: I cannot speak what I feel. I just know the longing to be
in your presence, to know that you are with me always.
I cannot leave your presence. I long to carry that with
me in my deepest core.

JESUS: Tonight, as you prepare for bed and in your sleeping,
practice that very knowing. I *am* with you.

During the night I hear the words "be with me" over and over.
With the rhythm of my breath I also hear "I am the vine and you
are the branches," "I in Thee and Thou in me." The rhythm of
the words moves in and out like gentle waves during my rest.

In the morning I walk and the words continue within. A coun-
terpoint of thoughts also begins: yesterday's judgments about not
being fully present to clients and friends. I was not available in
the way I want to be. I was conserving my energy. I recognized
my depletion and my need for rest. As I walk, I notice a white
feather on my path. I pick it up and resume my dialogue.

JOAN: My walk is with you. My challenge is to trust my
knowing, living my way into the heart of the mystery
that you are. You who were before all things and yet
you are also here with me in my life, my work, my
walk—step-by-step.

JESUS: Be with me and I will be with you. Be with me, I *am*
with you.

I return from my walk with a few hours left until noon. In
preparation for return, I paint the view from the window in a small

sketch journal that I will keep near my desk. I will stand it open to that page as a reminder of my time apart and my perspective of gratitude for much that makes up my life in the village.

At noon I meditate, joining in spirit with the sisters at Trans-figuration Monastery as they chant and pray their noonday office. When I eat my lunch and begin to think of my return to family and work, I also savor my connection with the monastic rhythm of solitude and community.

My mind begins to move to listing things that I need to do and to questions about what's next. My thoughts go to the three women who will come tomorrow for a counseling session. They return to move together through the painful place that we left last time. How will we go deeper beneath the pain to touch the center where they join in their love for and commitment to each other?

I think of my manuscript waiting for me. Will my writing ever reach book form? How will I do it in the midst of all that makes up my days? As I feel my inner space begin to fill with anxious thoughts, I shift my focus to the process of writing, which I have loved, and all that I have learned about my own journey through writing this book. As I move from anxiety to gratitude, I feel an opening within, hospitable space for me to celebrate what I have learned.

As a student in the school for the education of the heart, I have found that I learn best by going deep in the familiar.

"The Benedictine Way" has opened new areas of learning for me. It is, in Sister Donald's words, "one of the great 'schools' for the education of the heart.... Balanced, humane, yet challenging, it calls us to return again and again to the Center of all centers, not to exclude but to integrate."[82]

In my life as a householder I have found that going deep in my daily experience is the way that I can apply the three vows which have been part of the Benedictine experience for centuries. They are becoming familiar to me now as I work with them: stability or "standing still in one's own center," openness to change or "availability," and listening to God. I recognize their potential as balancing components within the rhythms of my life.

I will always be a learner. The creative one, my learner, is at the core my being. At the center I am one with the Creator, the Center of all centers. I am a sacred mystery and I am learning to honor that mystery. My learning involves all my being. I continue to use the Celtic phrase, "my soul entire," to mean body, mind, emotions, intuition. For me the phrase encompasses all that goes into making me who I am. I want to become familiar with each of these modes of perception in order to tend the flame that is uniquely mine. Each mode provides a way for me to grow in my ability to listen to God as I seek to live in a more balanced way.

One of my challenges as a learner is to recognize when I begin to lose my balance. There are signs, flags, signals that precede imbalance and loss of equilibrium. I need to honor those signs and respond before I get pulled off center. This brings me back to the practices that help me to tend the flame so that I can maintain my balance and inner stability when outer events are unstable and constantly changing.

These are my current practices—early morning walking, meditation, living with a psalm, praying for others, and opening myself to the guidance of the Holy Spirit for the concerns that I carry. I read short spiritual writings and take time in the forest to do my soul work. The process of assimilating, distilling, integrating, and celebrating life experience does take time.

To keep my balance I also need to take time apart for a day with no agenda. As with these last twenty-four hours, time unfolded and defined itself. When I finally reach the still pool of solitude through my various practices, I am enabled to rest in God and listen with a receptive heart. This contemplative experience I call inner hospitality. I carry it with me as I return to the village. It helps me extend hospitality to others.

The process of returning is important in itself. I need to create rituals at home that bridge from my time apart. My early morning ritual of lighting a candle before I begin to write connects me with my love of the surrounding darkness. I am once again in forest time. When that time of deep stillness comes to an end, I am mindful as I blow out the candle.

> Candlelight
> transition
> from the night
> of empty space
> to
> bird call
> and the dawn
> I extinguish you
> my silent companion
> letting go
> once more
> of
> this
> most sacred time.

I have learned that it is important to allow for conscious transitions from forest time. People find different ways to do this. A woman on a retreat anticipated her transition to home life by deciding to use her train commute in a new way. She traveled several times a week through Lancaster County in Pennsylvania to New York to teach in a college. During the period of time that the train passed through Amish country, she chose to put aside her course work in order to sketch mindfully, focusing on the simplicity of line and view. Another woman has found ways to make a transition from desert solitude to her life in community.

Since I currently live in New England, it is difficult to get to the desert often. When I can't, I have reminders at home; an adobe candleholder I made from desert clay, poems I have written, and collages made while on retreats. I realize that being there has helped me access my creative spirit, too. These objects guide me back to desert time and I feel gratitude. I can have desert solitude wherever I am—times that renew and replenish me, giving me sustenance for the work ahead.

I will always be a learner in my work life. This morning I am grateful in particular for the three women with whom I will meet tomorrow. They each are angels with boots on, living their lives by being very present and grounded in the realities of their unique situations. At the same time, each in her own way is open to the Divine at work in the midst of her losses and pain. I am learning so much from them in our work of going deep in the familiar together.

Going deep in the familiar also applies to the way that I have discovered language for my spiritual journey. As with holy sites where a Christian cathedral has been built on a Celtic sacred mound, or over a spring once known to the ancients as a "womb opening of the earth Mother,"[83] there are levels and levels to expressing the inexpressible. I begin my exploration with my own experience as a pilgrim on the way. I enter through the words of my religious heritage. I also explore beneath them to earlier words and experiences of the holy. Deeply touched by the experiences of others, I finally move to the wordless realm of silence and mystery.

In this process I have come to know my ultimate dependence on the Divine, the deep underground river of life-giving water that replenishes, upholds, and guides me. In my early twenties I wrote these words: Oh, God, you are to me a wide, flowing, deep, clear, gentle but powerful River....

When I was in my thirties, one summer night I went swimming. While I was in the water it began to rain. I do not know how long it lasted. I was in forest time, not linear time. What I do know was that I was fully present. Later that night I was wakened with words and music for a song. I had never written a song before, but I put the words to paper. The music did not leave me.

> Underneath, around me,
>   beneath and coming down on me,
> Wind, water, rain.
> Then opening above me,
>   dancing all around me,
> Wind, water, rain.
>
> Your welcoming acceptance,
>   deep stillness as I plunge to you,
> Wind, Water, Rain.
> Your breath and spirit gentle,
>   then surging, reeling, touching,
> Wind, water rain.
>
> I am in the midst of you,
>   Your elemental presence feel
> Wind, water, rain.
> I am but a part of you
>   I know you as I live in you,
> Wind, water, rain.

Water continues to be a reminder of Divine Presence. This summer we slept next to the brook in a camper for several nights. I became aware that I did not always hear the sound of water flowing, even though it was always there. Then when I brought my attention to it, listening with full presence, the sound filled the space around and within me.

I awaken again to this truth: To be aware of the Presence—the ever present stream of Living Water, flowing through my being, my life, the life of my loved ones, the human family, and all creation— is the purpose of spiritual practice. I celebrate this knowing as I journey toward home, seeking to live my way into the heart of mystery, day-by-day, step-by-step.

As I gather up my things to return to my home in the village, I pick up the white feather that I found on my path this morning. Holding it in my hand, I bow in this sacred space that has welcomed me. "Thank you," I say. "Thank you."

Reflection

1. Reflect on your experience of "village life," your community at this time in your life.

2. Be aware of people, creatures, sacred places, and practices that support you.

3. Take time to express your gratitude.

NOTES

1. Christine Downing, *Journey through Menopause* (New York: Crossroad, 1987), 26.

2. Allan Chinen, *In the Ever After: Fairy Tales and the Second Half of Life* (Wilmette, Ill.: Chiron Publications, 1992), 60.

3. Sister Donald Corcoran, "Reflections on the Monastic Spiritual Journey," *Word and Spirit: A Monastic Review* 15 (1993): 13.

4. Jean Baker Miller, "The Development of Women's Sense of Self," *Woman Growth in Connection: Writings from the Stone Center* (New York: Guilford Press, 1991), 13–14. "Being-in-relation" is the term used by Jean Baker Miller to describe the "early interacting sense of self which is present for infants of both sexes."

5. Ira Progoff, *At a Journal Workshop* (New York: Dialogue House, 1975), 95.

6. Esther de Waal, *God under My Roof: Celtic Songs and Blessings* (Oxford: SLG Press, 1994), 15.

7. Ibid., 7.

8. Ibid., 17.

9. John O'Donohue, *Anam Cara: Wisdom from the Celtic World,* Sounds True audiocassette FO39, 1996. From his tape "Aging: The Beauty of the Inner Harvest."

10. Thomas Merton, *The Sign of Jonas* (New York: Harcourt, Brace, 1953), 207.

11. Joan Chittister, *The Rule of St. Benedict: Insight for the Ages* (New York: Crossroad, 1995), 32—adapted story.

12. Thich Nhat Hanh, *Peace in Every Step: The Path of Mindfulness in Everyday Life* (New York: Bantam Books, 1991), 8.

13. R. Cameron Borton, monograph, "Guidelines for Christian Meditation," 1990.

14. See John Main, *Word into Silence* (New York: Paulist Press, 1981) and Laurence Freeman, *Christian Meditation: Your Daily Practice* (Rydalmere NSW 2116, Australia: Hunt and Thorpe, 1994).

15. *The Rule of Taizé* (Taizé, France: Les Presses de Taizé, 1961), 22.

189

16. Chinen, *In the Ever After*, 60.

17. Edith Sullwold, Ph.D., in conversation.

18. Esther de Waal, *A Seven Day Journey with Thomas Merton* (Ann Arbor, Mich.: Servant Publications, 1992), 17.

19. Chittister, *Rule of St. Benedict*, 148.

20. Two books by Esther de Waal that have been helpful are *Seeking God: The Way of St. Benedict* (Collegeville, Minn.: Liturgical Press, 1984), and *Living with Contradiction: Reflections on the Rule of St. Benedict* (San Francisco: Harper & Row, 1989).

21. de Waal, *Living with Contradiction*, 48–52.

22. Sam Keen, *Gabriel Marcel* (Richmond, Va.: John Knox Press, 1967), 26–27.

23. Joe McCown, *Availability: Gabriel Marcel and the Phenomenon of Human Openness* (Missoula, Mont.: Scholars Press for the American Academy of Religion, 1978), 27.

24. May Sarton, *Journal of a Solitude* (New York: W. W. Norton, 1973), 150.

25. de Waal, *Seeking God*, 58.

26. de Waal, *Living with Contradiction*, 49.

27. Sister Donald Corcoran, O.S.B., Ph.D., from a retreat talk on Soul and Spirit at the oblate meeting, Transfiguration Monastery, March 1995.

28. For some of us, "getting through it" is not really a choice, for it feels like the only option that we have. However, when that survival pattern becomes abusive for any party involved, the courageous and self-caring choice is to leave, to get out. Staying with an emotionally or physically abusive relationship is life-threatening for soul and body. Leaving becomes self-care in action rather than running away. It is a strong act of tending the sacredness of our whole being.

29. Ross Cannon, monograph written on the occasion of the fiftieth anniversary of marriage with Mary L. Cannon, September 1, 1984.

30. *Book of Common Prayer* (New York: Church Hymnal Corporation and Seabury Press, 1977), 133.

31. Renee Beck and Sidney Barbara Metrick, *The Art of Ritual: A Guide to Creating and Performing Your Own Rituals for Growth and Change* (Berkeley, Calif.: Celestial Arts, 1990), ii.

32. Elizabeth Yates, *Call It Zest* (Brattleboro, Vt.: Stephen Greene Press, 1977), 161.

33. de Waal, *Living with Contradiction*, 126.

34. de Waal, *Seeking God*, 69–70.

35. Ibid., 70.

36. Terry Tempest Williams, *Refuge: An Unnatural History of Family and Place* (New York: Vintage Books), 178.

37. See Andrew Canale, *Beyond Depression: A Practical Guide for Healing Despair* (Rockport, Mass.: Element, 1992), chap. 1.

38. Chittister, *Rule of St. Benedict*, 19.

39. Ibid., 20.

40. de Waal, *Seeking God*, 42–43.

41. Thomas Moore, "Care of the Soul," presentation at the Interface Conference on Mid-life, Watertown, Mass., March 1993.

42. Robert Gerzon, *Finding Serenity in the Age of Anxiety* (New York: Macmillan, 1997), chap. 5.

43. Ibid., 25–27.

44. Beverly Williams, excerpt from her poem "Solitude."

45. Kathleen Norris, *Little Girls in Church* (Pittsburgh: University of Pittsburgh Press, 1995), 54.

46. Beverly Williams, excerpt from her poem "Wilderness."

47. Sister Donald Corcoran, *Oblate Newsletter of the Camaldolese Benedictine Nuns* 1, no. 2 (Winter 1995).

48. Beverly Williams, excerpt from her poem "Solitude."

49. Edith Sullwold, Ph.D., in conversation.

50. Moore, "Care of the Soul," presentation.

51. Jean Shinoda Bolen, M.D., *Crossing to Avalon: A Woman's Midlife Pilgrimage* (New York: HarperSanFrancisco, 1994), 148–49.

52. Matthew Fox, *Meditations with Meister Eckhart* (Santa Fe, N.Mex.: Bear & Company, 1982), 45.

53. "The Great Yellowstone Fires," *The National Geographic* 175, no. 2 (February 1989): 258.

54. Sister Donald Corcoran, in conversation.

55. Bolen, *Crossing to Avalon*, 141.

56. Norris, *Little Girls in Church*, 54.

57. Williams, excerpt from her poem "Wilderness," written as a reflection after reading this chapter.

58. Gabriel Lusser Rico, *Writing the Natural Way: Using Right-Brain Techniques to Release Your Expressive Powers* (Los Angeles: J. P. Tarcher, 1983).

59. Dan Seeger, Executive Director of Pendle Hill, in conversation, May 1994.

60. Corcoran, *Oblate Newsletter.*

61. Sam Keen, *Gabriel Marcel* (Richmond, Va.: John Knox Press, 1967), 21.

62. Diogenes Allen, *Temptation* (Cambridge, Mass.: Cowley Publications, 1986), 18.

63. Chinen, *In the Ever After*, 141.

64. Ibid., 30.

65. May Sarton, *The House by the Sea: A Journal* (New York: W. W. Norton, 1977), 25.

66. Benedict of Nursia, Italy (A.D. 480–547) wrote the Rule and established many monasteries before the divisions within the church. His life and work preceded the spilt between the Orthodox and the Roman Catholic Church, the Anglican Communion, and the Protestant Reformation. Brigid of Ireland (450-523) founded a community for women in Kildare and was ordained in the manner that bishops are now ordained. When Bishop Mel lay hands upon her he claimed, " 'I have no power in this matter. God has ordained Brigid.' " This story is from *Celtic Night Prayer*, compiled by the members of the Northumbria Community (London: Marshall Pickering, 1996), 22.

67. Gabriel Uhlein, *Meditations with Hildegard of Bingen* (Santa Fe, N.Mex.: Bear & Company, 1982), 45.

68. de Waal, *A Seven Day Journey with Thomas Merton*, 5.

69. Thomas Keating, "The Method of Centering Prayer," Contemplative Outreach Limited, *www.centeringprayer.com/methodcp.htm*, 1995.

70. Clarissa Pinkola Estés, Ph.D., *Women Who Run with the Wolves: Myths and Stories of the Wild Woman Archetype* (New York: Ballantine, 1992), 269.

71. Norvene Vest, *No Moment Too Small: Rhythms of Silence, Prayer, and Holy Reading* (Boston: Cowley Publications, 1994). For further exploration of the practice of *lectio divina*, this is a very encouraging book written by an Episcopal laywoman.

72. Gunilla Norris, *Being Home: A Book of Meditations* (New York: Bell Tower, 1991), xiii.

73. de Waal, *A Seven Day Journey with Thomas Merton*, 17.

74. Keen, *Gabriel Marcel*, 5.

75. Katherine Howard, O.S.B., *Praying with Benedict* (Winona, Minn.: St. Mary's Press 1996), chap. 14, 110–15.

76. Sister Donald Corcoran, in conversation.

77. For further information about Wellspring House the following book by Rosemary Haughton tells the continuing story: *Song in a Strange Land: The Wellspring Story and the Homelessness of Women* (Springfield, Ill.: Templegate Publishers, 1990). See also the article on Wellspring House by Rebecca Koch, Mary Lewis, and Wendy Quinones in *Mothering at the Margins: Voices of Resistance* (Boston: Guilford Press, 1998).

78. Rosemary Haughton, "A Time for Grieving, Rejoicing," *Gloucester Daily Times*, "My View" column, April 12, 1997.

79. *Doula* is a Greek word used for an experienced woman who is a supportive companion and reassuring presence to a mother during labor and delivery. Research is presented in Marshall Klaus, John Kennell, and Phyllis Klaus, *Mothering the Mother: A Doula Can Help You Have a Shorter, Easier and Healthier Birth* (Reading, Mass.: Addison-Wesley, 1993).

80. Sister Donald Corcoran, O.S.B., Ph.D., from a retreat talk on Soul and Spirit at the oblate meeting, Transfiguration Monastery, March 1995.

81. Haughton, "A Time for Grieving, Rejoicing."

82. Corcoran, "Reflections on the Monastic Spiritual Journey," 13.

83. Joan C. Borton, *Drawing from the Women's Well: Reflections on the Life Passage of Menopause* (San Diego, Calif.: LuraMedia, 1991), xvi.

BIBLIOGRAPHY

Allen, Diogenes. *Temptation.* Cambridge, Mass.: Cowley Publications, 1986.

Beck, Renee, and Sidney Barbara Metrick. *The Art of Ritual: A Guide to Creating and Performing Your Own Rituals for Growth and Change.* Berkeley, Calif.: Celestial Arts, 1990.

Bolen, Jean Shinoda. *Crossing to Avalon: A Woman's Midlife Pilgrimage.* New York: HarperSanFrancisco, 1994.

Borton, Joan C. *Drawing from the Women's Well: Reflections on the Life Passage of Menopause.* San Diego, Calif.: LuraMedia, 1992.

Borton, R. Cameron. Monograph, "On Christian Meditation," 1988.

Canale, Andrew. *Beyond Depression: A Practical Guide for Healing Despair.* Rockport, Mass.: Element, 1992.

Cannon, Ross. Monograph, on the occasion of the fiftieth anniversary of marriage with Mary L. Cannon, September 1, 1984.

Chinen, Allan. *In the Ever After: Fairy Tales and the Second Half of Life.* Wilmette, Ill.: Chiron Publications, 1992.

Chittister, Joan. *The Rule of St. Benedict: Insights for the Ages.* New York: Crossroad, 1995.

Corcoran, Sister Donald. *Oblate Newsletter of the Camaldolese Benedictine Nuns* 1, no. 2 (Winter 1995).

———. "Reflections on the Monastic Spiritual Journey," *Word and Spirit: A Monastic Review* 15 (1993): 12–29.

de Waal, Esther. *God under My Roof: Celtic Songs and Blessings.* Oxford, England: SLG Press, 1994.

———. *Living with Contradiction: Reflections on the Rule of St. Benedict.* San Francisco: Harper & Row, 1989.

———. *Seeking God: The Way of St. Benedict.* Collegeville, Minn.: Liturgical Press, 1984.

———. *A Seven Day Journey with Thomas Merton.* Ann Arbor, Mich.: Servant Publications, 1992.

Downing, Christine. *Journey through Menopause.* New York: Crossroad, 1987.

Episcopal Church. *Book of Common Prayer.* New York: Church Hymnal Corporation and Seabury Press, 1977.

Estés, Clarissa Pinkola. *Women Who Run with the Wolves: Myths and Stories of the Wild Woman Archetype.* New York: Ballantine, 1992.

Fox, Matthew. *Meditations with Meister Eckhart.* Santa Fe, N.Mex.: Bear & Company, 1982.

Gerzon, Robert. *Finding Serenity in the Age of Anxiety.* New York: Macmillan, 1997.

Gomes, Peter J. *The Good Book.* New York: William Morrow, 1996.

Haughton, Rosemary. *Song in a Strange Land: The Wellspring Story and the Homelessness of Women.* Springfield, Ill.: Templegate Publishers, 1990.

———. "A Time for Grieving, Rejoicing." *Gloucester Daily Times,* "My View" column, April 12, 1997.

Howard, Sister Katherine. *Praying with Benedict.* Winona, Minn.: St. Mary's Press, 1996.

Keating, Thomas. "The Method of Centering Prayer." Contemplative Outreach Limited. *www.centeringprayer.com/methodcp.htm,* 1995.

Keen, Sam. *Gabriel Marcel.* Richmond, Va.: John Knox Press, 1967.

Klaus, Marshall, John Kennell, and Phyllis Klaus. *Mothering the Mother.* Reading, Mass.: Addison-Wesley, 1993.

Main, John. *Moment of Christ.* London: Darton, Longman & Todd, 1991.

———. *Word into Silence.* New York: Paulist Press, 1981.

Miller, Jean Baker. "The Development of Women's Sense of Self." In Judith V. Jordan et al. *Woman's Growth in Connection: Writings from the Stone Center.* New York: Guilford Press, 1991.

Moore, Thomas. *Care of the Soul: A Guide for Cultivating Depth and Sacredness in Everyday Life.* New York: HarperCollins, 1992.

Nhat Hanh, Thich. *Peace in Every Step: The Path of Mindfulness in Everyday Life.* New York: Bantam Books, 1991.

Norris, Gunilla. *Being Home: A Book of Meditations.* New York: Bell Tower, 1991.

Norris, Kathleen. *Little Girls in Church.* Pittsburgh: University of Pittsburgh Press, 1995.

———. *Dakota: A Spiritual Geography.* New York: Ticknor and Fields, 1993.

———. *The Cloister Walk.* New York: Riverhead Books, 1996.

Northumbria Community, eds. *Celtic Night Prayer.* London: Marshall Pickering, 1996.

O'Donohue, John. *Anam Cara: Wisdom from the Celtic World.* Sounds True audiocassette FO39, 1996.

Progoff, Ira. *At a Journal Workshop.* New York: Dialogue House, 1975.

Sarton, May. *The House by the Sea.* New York: W. W. Norton, 1977.

————. *May: Journal of a Solitude.* New York: W. W. Norton, 1992.

Taizé Community. *The Rule of Taizé.* Taizé, France: Les Presses de Taizé, 1961.

Uhlein, Gabriel. *Meditations with Hildegard of Bingen.* Santa Fe, N.Mex.: Bear & Company, 1982.

Vest, Norvene. *No Moment Too Small: Rhythms of Silence, Prayer, and Holy Reading.* Boston: Cowley Publications, 1994.

Williams, Terry Tempest. *Refuge: An Unnatural History of Family and Place.* New York: Random House, 1991.

Yates, Elizabeth. *Call It Zest.* Brattleboro, Vt.: Stephen Greene Press, 1977.

OTHER BOOKS FROM PILGRIM PRESS

My Mother Prayed for Me:
Faith Journaling for African American Women
LaVerne McCain Gill
0-8298-1396-9/cloth/104 pages/$14.95

How do you develop the discipline of writing a faith journal? Gill provides guidance to African American women in particular and women in general on writing and recording their spiritual witness. A five-step process for journaling that focuses on the stories of the Bible and personal witnesses to God's presence in contemporary life is shared.

Celebrating Her: Feminist Ritualizing Comes of Age
Wendy Hunter Roberts
Foreword by Marjorie Proctor Smith
0-8298-1258-X/paper/160 pages/$15.95

"*Celebrating Her* truly expresses 'feminist ritualizing come of age.' Here we find a mature transformative vision in which ancient roots and contemporary critique come together. . . . For those seeking guidance in the creation of celebrative community, this is an indispensable resource."
— Rosemary Radford Ruether, Professor of Applied Theology,
Garrett-Evangelical Theological Seminary

Celebrating Her is a feminist exploration and analysis of eight rites and celebrations of the emerging goddess-centered women's spirituality movement. This is a vital resource for those investigating more holistic, inclusive worship.

Wisdom's Daughters: Stories of the Women around Jesus
Elizabeth G. Watson
0-8298-1221-0/184 pages/paper/$12.95

Wisdom Daughter's tells the life of Jesus through the eyes and hearts of fourteen New Testament women. Readers can visualize Jesus calling these women to follow him and become the bearers of his message when all of the disciples except John deserted him.

Doing the Twist to Amazing Grace
Alice Ogden Bellis
0-8298-1273-3/128 pages/paper/$9.95

Often humorous, always engaging, Bellis shares her personal experiences and keen biblical insights to help active worshipers as well as those reentering the church to gather up their faith experiences and faith understanding—and leads them to deeper, more mature expressions of faith. Study questions are included for reflection and discussion.

To order these or any other books
from The Pilgrim Press
call or write to:

The Pilgrim Press
700 Prospect Avenue East
Cleveland, Ohio 44115-1100

Phone orders: 1-800-537-3394 • Fax orders: 216-736-2206
Please include shipping charges of $3.50 for the first book
and $0.50 for each additional book.
Or order from our websites at
www.pilgrimpress.com and www.ucpress.com.

Prices subject to change without notice.